The
Gluten-Free Almond Flour
Cookbook

the GLUTEN-FREE ALMOND FLOUR *cookbook*

Breakfasts, Entrées, and More

Elana Amsterdam

Photographs by Annabelle Breakey

CELESTIAL ARTS
Berkeley

Published in the United States by Celestial Arts, an imprint of the Crown Publishing Group,
a division of Random House, Inc., New York.
www.crownpublishing.com
www.tenspeed.com

Celestial Arts and the Celestial Arts colophon are registered trademarks of Random House, Inc.

Library of Congress Cataloging-in-Publication Data

Amsterdam, Elana.
  The gluten-free almond flour cookbook / Elana Amsterdam ; photographs by Annabelle
Breakey.
      p. cm.
  Includes index.
  Summary: "A collection of 99 gluten-free, quick-and-healthy whole foods recipes using
almond flour"—Provided by publisher.
  1. Gluten-free diet—Recipes. 2. Cookery (Almonds) I. Title.
  RM237.86.A47 2009
  641.5'638—dc22
                          2008055172
ISBN 978-1-58761-345-6

Printed in China

Cover and text design by Betsy Stromberg
Food styling by Dan Becker
Prop styling by Emma Star Jensen
Food stylist assistant: Lena Hung

10 9 8 7 6 5

First Edition

Dedication

For Rob, an honest critic, amazing friend, and fantastic partner; J, for sharing your exquisitely discerning palate and truthfulness; and E, for knowing how to mix the wet into the dry.

Contents

Acknowledgments

So many thanks go to so many people for their help in putting together this cookbook. First, Rob, thanks for your patience, endless taste testing, and only spitting out samples that had ginger in them. To Helen, for hanging out in the kitchen with me for the past twenty-five years. To Marylyn, for the endless conversations, dreaming, and inspiration. To Alison Schwartz at ICM, for taking the leap and being there every step of the way. To Lucy Rosset, for encouragement and caring during challenging times. And finally, to Elaine Gottschall, for introducing me to the world of almond flour.

Introduction

$\mathcal{I}$'ve always loved to cook. As a girl, I baked cookies almost every day after school—by the time I was twelve, I had the Tollhouse recipe committed to memory. In high school, I created my own chocolate chip cookie recipe and sold the treats locally.

In my midtwenties, I spent my waking hours at a full-time job in environmental consulting and taught yoga on the side. Part of my yoga teacher training included the study of Ayurvedic nutrition. My lifelong interest in cooking—albeit not exactly wholesome up to that point—combined with my passion for ecological matters resulted in my thorough investigation of nutrition and alternative living, which changed the course of my life.

At age thirty, my interest in healthy eating and holistic living proved pivotal when I was diagnosed with celiac disease, an autoimmune disorder that causes damage to the small intestine, which can lead to the malabsorption of nutrients. This genetic intolerance to gluten, a protein found in wheat, rye, and barley, triggers a destructive reaction of the immune system. Celiac, which often goes undiagnosed, is considered a multiorgan system disease.[1]

This diagnosis led me on a personal culinary journey to develop delicious, nourishing, gluten-free foods for everyone in my home. I had no interest in creating separate meal plans for various family members. My intention was to make one meal that would meet my dietary restrictions without compromising taste for family and friends.

As I explored the gluten-free world, I was disappointed. I could not get accustomed to the dry, odd-flavored baked goods and strange, gritty textures. I wouldn't compromise taste just because I had celiac disease.

In addition, I found that much of the (overly sweetened) high-glycemic, gluten-free foods played with my blood sugar in an alarming way. For me, mood swings and high-carb hangovers were unacceptable side effects of a gluten-free diet.

Luckily, I stumbled upon an enlightened group of gluten-free people on the Internet; these people introduced me to almond flour, which I quickly saw had great potential for creating classic recipes that were gluten-free, high in protein, and lower in sugar and carbohydrates.

After three years of tasting and testing—on classes of schoolchildren (trust me, they won't lie—if the food isn't good, they'll just spit it out), friends, family, and complete strangers—I began to feel encouraged in my mission to turn gluten-free food into delicious mainstream fare.

It wasn't long before parents stopped me in the parking lot with recipe requests. I mailed recipes to friends and family across the country. And the best part was that most of these people didn't have food restrictions.

Soon I had the problems that every recipe writer wants: moms calling me to bake their children's birthday cakes, friends and acquaintances asking for cooking classes, teachers requesting my recipes for school parties. In response, I launched a blog in 2006 (www.elanaspantry.com) to share my recipes, health tips, and overall love affair with food with a broader audience.

Almond flour has been the perfect vehicle in my journey to unite people around good food. It is a simple ingredient—easy to use, with elegant results and excellent nutrition. I hope you enjoy making these recipes as much as I have enjoyed creating them! I offer the fruits of my labor with love and gratitude to friends, family, and readers.

Using Almond Flour

*I*n European countries where wheat and corn don't dominate agriculture, vibrant, centuries-old traditions make delicious use of almond flour in dishes such as marzipan, macaroons, and tortes. These cultures discovered the secret of almond flour long ago: it tastes delicious, it's easy to use, and it's a superfood.

TASTE

Almond flour tastes sweet, rich, and buttery, making it somewhat indistinguishable from wheat flour in baked goods and other dishes.

As opposed to the dry, gritty texture of rice flour and other gluten-free flours in baked goods, almond flour is smooth and has excellent mouth feel.

EASE OF USE

Almond flour is as easy to use as wheat flour and much less tedious than complex gluten-free flours, which require numerous supplemental ingredients such as xanthum gum, cornstarch, and potato flakes for binding purposes. Because it requires numerous additional ingredients, gluten-free baking has traditionally been known as a painstaking, time-consuming task. This is not the case with almond flour baking, which is actually even quicker and easier than most traditional wheat-based recipes that require yeast and rising time.

SUPERFOOD

Almond flour is a highly nutritious superfood that is low-carb and rich in vitamins, minerals, and "good" fats. Almond flour is not only the healthiest flour around, it is also higher in protein and far richer in nutrients than wheat flour and its gluten-free counterparts; a serving of almond flour is packed with protein and fiber.

Comparison of Nutritional Values: Almond Flour versus Other Flours

Nutrition Info (100 g)	Protein	Carbohydrates	Glycemic Index[2]	Fiber
Almond Flour[3]	21.94 g	19.44 g	< 1	10.4 g
White Wheat Flour[4]	9.71 g	76.22 g	71	2.4 g
Rice Flour[5]	5.95 g	80.13 g	98	2.4 g

Almond flour is not only full of incredible antioxidants and found to be allergenic in only 1 percent of the population, it is also an ideal recovery food for cyclists and other athletes.

Vitamins and Minerals: Almond Flour versus Other Flours

Nutrition Info (100 g)	Almond Flour[6]	White Wheat Flour[7]	Rice Flour[8]
Potassium	687 mg	149 mg	76 mg
Magnesium	275 mg	25 mg	35 mg
Niacin	3.6 mg	1.2 mg	2.6 mg
Alpha-tocopherol	24.7 mg	.05 mg	.11 mg
Calcium	216 mg	20 mg	10 mg
Iron	3.72 mg	1.26 mg	.35 mg

During the 1990s, the medical community began to discover the health benefits of almonds; numerous studies now point to increasing almond intake as beneficial for stabilizing blood sugar, controlling appetite, preventing obesity, and providing antioxidants as well as numerous other nutrients. Such studies also tout almonds as a heart-healthy food.

Unlike its high-glycemic wheat and rice flour counterparts, the high protein content of almond flour makes it an optimal ingredient for stabilizing blood sugar. It is thus the ideal fare for diabetics and those who experience difficulty metabolizing sugar, which is a common issue among people with celiac disease.

Recent research indicates that diabetics and those with celiac disease share a similar strand of DNA, enhancing the appeal of almond flour as a tool to simultaneously go gluten-free while lowering one's glucose intake. The recipes in this book use almond flour and low-glycemic sweeteners rather than sugar, allowing people with food restrictions to enjoy their favorite desserts without worrying about spiking blood sugar levels.

Because almonds enhance satiety, they are an ideal food for those looking to maintain or lose weight. Researchers concluded that almonds' heart-healthy monounsaturated fat helps to satisfy appetite and prevent overeating. A 2003 study in the *Journal of Obesity* found that "adding a daily ration of almonds to a low-calorie diet enhanced weight loss as well as significantly improved risk factors associated with heart disease."

The American Heart Association has further determined that the "good" fats in almonds actually lower cholesterol, making almonds a star ingredient for patients with heart disease.

Finally, there is no reason for almond flour to be limited to the above populations on special diets. Almond flour provides a return to wholesome eating in an era of increasingly processed food, proliferating food allergies, and health ailments. As you will see in the following recipes, almond flour is the king of alternative flours.

Stocking the Almond Flour Pantry

*T*he recipes in this book are simple and easy—some contain six ingredients or less, and can be prepared in well under an hour. You do not need to be a chef, or even have prior cooking experience, to successfully prepare the dishes featured here. Though it is crucial that you have the correct ingredients. In this chapter, you'll find information about the ingredients featured in the recipes, as well as handling and storing instructions.

ALMOND FLOUR

Almond flour is actually a by-product of the process in which almond slices and slivers are produced. First, the almonds are blanched—the skin is removed in a water bath. Next, they are cut into sliced or diced almonds. The fragments and small pieces that result from this process (a sort of almond sawdust) ultimately become almond flour. In the final stage of this process, the by-product, which may be somewhat coarse, is put through a screen with tiny holes to ensure smooth flour with a uniformly fine consistency.

   Almond flour is not to be confused with almond meal, which contains whole, ground almonds that still have the skin on them. *Please note:* Almond meal or almond flour that is not blanched will not work for the recipes in this book—you will not achieve the desired results.

Baking with almond flour is extremely easy. There is no yeast or rising time with the baked goods in this cookbook, which means instant gratification in your baking endeavors.

Almond flour is available at health food stores and many grocery stores as well. It is also widely available on the Internet. I recommend purchasing almond flour online, as it is generally half the price of the same product in a retail outlet.

Please note: Unfortunately, the almond flour produced by Bob's Red Mill is much coarser than the other brands of almond flour I have tested for this book. Because of its consistency it does not work in these recipes.

Whenever possible, purchase your almond flour from a vendor that refrigerates it. The product will be of higher quality because the fats are less likely to have gone rancid and therefore it will keep for a longer period of time. Almond flour can be stored in a tightly sealed glass jar in the refrigerator or freezer for several months.

SALT

I use Celtic Sea Salt in all of my recipes and highly recommend it. Be sure to purchase the *finely ground* Celtic Sea Salt as it is optimal for baking—it mixes into cookies and other baked goods quite evenly.

I store my salt in a large glass jar in the pantry, where it keeps indefinitely and requires no cold storage. I also keep a small bowl of salt on the counter next to my measuring spoons, so I have some ready when I'm cooking up a quick batch of cookies or other treats.

AGAVE NECTAR

Sweetness is the first taste we experience in life, the primal taste of infancy; we all need some form of sweetness in our lives. For several years, I researched delicious, healthy alternatives to sugar that held up well in the baking process yet did not substantially raise glycemic index values.

Because celiac and diabetes ride on the same gene (increasing the frequency of one disease when the other occurs), I have found it helpful as someone with celiac disease to monitor my intake of sweets. I do not believe that such diseases suddenly appear; I think they take years to develop and that anything we can do to lower our chances of incurring them is beneficial. For this reason, I have included a sweetness indicator in many of these recipes. It will let you know which recipes to use when you are in the mood for a slightly sweet treat or a more decadent dessert. Recipes that do not have a significant amount of sweetener do not have a sweetness indicator.

Agave, the nectar of the agave plant—a golden liquid readily available at health food stores—has become my go-to sweetener. It is much lower on the glycemic index than other sweeteners:

Glycemic Index

Sugar	58[9]
Maple Syrup	54[10]
Honey	52[11]
Agave Nectar	32[12]

In all of my recipes, I use USDA-certified organic light agave nectar. As opposed to dark or amber, light agave has a more neutral flavor and resembles sugar most closely in taste when added to baked goods.

Many people ask why I don't use honey as a sweetener in my recipes. I choose agave nectar because I consider honey a flavor, not a sweetener, and I tend to use it for medicinal purposes rather than as an ingredient in my baking.

I purchase agave nectar by the gallon because it dramatically cuts the cost. If you buy yours this way, be sure to also purchase a pump for the gallon-size container. Whatever you do, because of the expense, avoid buying small containers of agave.

GRAPESEED OIL

Let's face it, food needs fat to taste good; oils impart rich flavor and texture. Grapeseed is my oil of choice.

Why? Grapeseed oil is the ideal replacement for butter in baked goods, making it optimal for those on a dairy-free diet. It is also low in cholesterol, and has a neutral flavor.

I purchase my oils (including grapeseed) in glass containers, because plastic contains endocrine-disrupting chemicals that are exacerbated when they come into contact with oil.

COCONUT OIL

I use coconut oil to lend a tropical flavor to certain baked goods. At colder temperatures, coconut oil is solid and requires melting before it can be used in recipes. When heated, it can scorch very easily, so be sure to heat it at a very low temperature. During the summer months, it will be in a more liquid state and will not require melting. Purchase only food-grade coconut oil in glass jars, and make sure it is unrefined and not hydrogenated. High-quality coconut oil will have a slightly sweet smell, coconut flavor, and no aftertaste.

VANILLA EXTRACT

I use a high-quality pure organic gluten-free vanilla extract, manufactured by Flavorganics. I purchase the eight-ounce size, the largest sold retail, to reduce costs and minimize my consumption of glass.

CHOCOLATE

Chocolate is reputedly an aphrodisiac. In addition, studies show that chocolate is a potent antioxidant that can reduce blood pressure and raise good cholesterol. These benefits are derived from eating dark chocolate, not milk or white chocolate.

I bake with Dagoba organic unsweetened cocoa powder and dark chocolate (bars or chocodrops) because Dagoba is organic and dark chocolate has a much higher cocoa content and less sugar than semisweet or milk chocolate. The chocodrops are disks that are similar to chocolate chips, just a bit larger and flatter. If you want to use a bar of chocolate, just chop it into chunks and then measure it in a cup. If you are weighing the chocolate, one cup of chocodrops is equal to approximately six ounces by weight.

Because the percentages of cocoa butter and powder vary from product to product and brand to brand, make sure that the chocolate you use is 73 percent cacao for these recipes.

ARROWROOT POWDER

Arrowroot is a ubiquitous weed that grows in the southern United States. It is a thickener commonly used in Ayurvedic cooking.

If you are unfamiliar with arrowroot powder, the following basic tips will help. When a recipe calls for an arrowroot slurry or paste, be sure to combine the arrowroot and water in a small bowl, making a smooth mixture without any lumps. Generally, you will be adding the slurry or paste to a mixture on the stove. When doing so, it is important to raise the heat to high and mix thoroughly until the arrowroot is well integrated and the mixture on the stove completely thickens.

AGAR FLAKES

Agar is a vegan thickener made of seaweed, similar to gelatin, commonly used in Asian cooking. When using this thickener it is of utmost importance to bring your mixture to a rolling boil, until the agar thoroughly dissolves.

FRUIT SPREAD

I use Rigoni di Asiago brand fruit spread, which is made from organic fruit. The fact that these fruit spreads are juice sweetened (with no refined sugars) adds to their appeal. When using jam, it's extremely important to use an organic product. In conventional jams, as the fruit concentrates so does the pesticide content. This creates an added toxic burden in little jam-loving children who weigh less than adults.

YACON SYRUP

Yacon is a root composed primarily of water and fructo-oligosaccharides (FOS)—these types of short chain sugars have a lower caloric value (as they are digested anaerobically) and high fiber content. I use yacon syrup in recipes that traditionally call for molasses, such as gingerbread.

ALL PURPOSE CHEF'S SHAKE SEASONING

This gluten-free spice blend produced by Spice Hunter contains onion, garlic, celery seed, marjoram, and several other ground spices. I use it as a convenient shortcut to add flavor to savory dishes rather than using a laundry list of spices.

MAGIC LINE LOAF PAN (7.5 by 3.5 by 2.25 inches)

This commercial quality, heavy-duty loaf pan is the perfect size for evenly cooking a loaf of bread made with almond flour. In my testing I found that standard size loaf pans did not bake the bread through to the center, leaving the middle undercooked. This loaf pan is shallow enough that your breads will be cooked through.

Breakfast

Banana Blueberry Muffins

MAKES 12 MUFFINS ❖ SWEETNESS: LOW

While I use agave nectar in many recipes, fruit alone sweetens these muffins, making them the ideal treat for those looking to reduce their glycemic load.

3 cups blanched almond flour

1/4 teaspoon sea salt

1 1/2 teaspoons baking soda

2 tablespoons grapeseed oil

3 large eggs

2 cups (4 to 5) mashed very ripe bananas

1 cup frozen blueberries

Preheat the oven to 350°F. Line 12 muffin cups with paper liners.

In a large bowl, combine the almond flour, salt, and baking soda. In a medium bowl, whisk together the grapeseed oil and eggs. Stir the wet ingredients into the almond flour mixture until thoroughly combined. Stir the bananas into the batter, then fold in the blueberries. Spoon the batter into the prepared muffin cups.

Bake for 35 to 40 minutes, until the muffin tops are golden brown and a toothpick inserted into the center of a muffin comes out clean. Let the muffins cool in the pan for 30 minutes, then serve.

Cinnamon Apple Muffins

MAKES 10 MUFFINS ✧ SWEETNESS: MEDIUM

A whisper of cinnamon and ambrosial bits of fresh apple scattered throughout make this moist, mouthwatering muffin great for breakfast, snack, or a healthy lunchbox treat.

2 cups blanched almond flour

1/2 teaspoon sea salt

1/2 teaspoon baking soda

1/4 cup arrowroot powder

1 teaspoon ground cinnamon

1/4 cup grapeseed oil

1/2 cup agave nectar

1 large egg

1 tablespoon vanilla extract

2 medium apples, peeled, cored, and diced into 1/4-inch cubes

Preheat the oven to 350°F. Line 10 muffin cups with paper liners.

In a large bowl, combine the almond flour, salt, baking soda, arrowroot powder, and cinnamon. In a medium bowl, whisk together the grapeseed oil, agave nectar, egg, and vanilla extract. Stir the wet ingredients into the almond flour mixture until thoroughly combined, then fold in the apples. Spoon the batter into the prepared muffin cups.

Bake for 30 to 35 minutes, until the muffin tops are golden brown and a toothpick inserted into the center of a muffin comes out clean. Let the muffins cool in the pan for 30 minutes, then serve.

Date Pecan Muffins

MAKES 12 MUFFINS ✧ SWEETNESS: MEDIUM

Satisfying and highly nutritious, these lightly sweetened muffins have chunks of date (a good source of potassium, calcium, and iron) and pecan (high in protein, fiber, and antioxidants) in every bite.

3 cups blanched almond flour

1/2 teaspoon sea salt

1/2 teaspoon baking soda

1/4 teaspoon ground nutmeg

1/4 cup grapeseed oil

2 tablespoons agave nectar

2 large eggs

1 tablespoon vanilla extract

2 medium apples, peeled, cored, and sliced

1 cup pecans, coarsely chopped

1/2 cup dates, chopped into 1/4-inch pieces

Preheat the oven to 350°F. Line 12 muffin cups with paper liners.

In a large bowl, combine the almond flour, salt, baking soda, and nutmeg. In a blender, combine the grapeseed oil, agave nectar, eggs, vanilla extract, and apples; process on high until smooth. Stir the wet ingredients into the almond flour mixture until thoroughly combined, then fold in the pecans and dates. Spoon the batter into the prepared muffin cups.

Bake for 35 to 45 minutes, until the muffin tops are golden brown and a toothpick inserted into the center of a muffin comes out clean. Let the muffins cool in the pan for 30 minutes, then serve.

Orange Apricot Scones

MAKES 16 SCONES ✦ SWEETNESS: MEDIUM

Unlike most scones, which tend to have chunks of dried fruit and nuts, the fruit in these scones is pureed, creating a uniquely smooth consistency. With a delicate orange-apricot flavor, you'll find that they are just too good to limit to breakfast.

3 cups blanched almond flour

1/4 teaspoon sea salt

3/4 teaspoon baking soda

1/2 teaspoon ground cinnamon

1/4 teaspoon ground nutmeg

1/4 cup grapeseed oil

3 tablespoons agave nectar

3 large eggs

1/2 cup dried apricots, chopped into 1/4-inch pieces

1/4 cup freshly squeezed orange juice

1 tablespoon orange zest

Preheat the oven to 350°F. Line 2 large baking sheets with parchment paper.

In a large bowl, combine the almond flour, salt, baking soda, cinnamon, and nutmeg. In a blender, combine the grapeseed oil, agave nectar, eggs, apricots, orange juice, and orange zest; process on high for about 1 minute, until smooth. Stir the wet ingredients into the almond flour mixture until thoroughly combined. Drop the batter, in scant 1/4 cups 2 inches apart, onto the prepared baking sheets.

Bake for 10 to 15 minutes, until golden brown or a toothpick inserted into the center of a scone comes out clean. Let the scones cool on the baking sheets for 30 minutes, then serve.

Chocolate Chip Scones

MAKES 16 SCONES ❖ SWEETNESS: MEDIUM

In college, I used to pretend chocolate chip scones were a breakfast food instead of a dessert, devouring one nearly every morning. Using agave nectar to lower the glycemic index of this scone makes my unique categorization less of a stretch. Rich in antioxidants and low in sugar, organic dark chocolate makes these decadent-looking scones a healthy indulgence.

2$^{1}/_{2}$ cups blanched almond flour

$^{1}/_{2}$ teaspoon sea salt

$^{1}/_{2}$ teaspoon baking soda

$^{1}/_{3}$ cup grapeseed oil

$^{1}/_{4}$ cup agave nectar

2 large eggs

1 cup coarsely chopped dark chocolate (73% cacao)

Preheat the oven to 350°F. Line 2 large baking sheets with parchment paper.

In a large bowl, combine the almond flour, salt, and baking soda. In a medium bowl, whisk together the grapeseed oil, agave nectar, and eggs. Stir the wet ingredients into the almond flour mixture until thoroughly combined, then fold in the chocolate. Drop the batter, in scant $^{1}/_{4}$ cups 2 inches apart, onto the prepared baking sheets.

Bake for 12 to 17 minutes, until golden brown or a toothpick inserted into the center of a scone comes out clean. Let the scones cool for 30 minutes on the baking sheets, then serve.

Classic Drop Biscuits

MAKES 8 BISCUITS ❖ SWEETNESS: LOW

These biscuits are simple to prepare and wonderfully versatile. They can either round out a savory, protein-filled breakfast or create a light summer dessert when used for Strawberry Shortcake (page 92) and are equally delicious served warm, right out of the oven.

2^1/$_2$ cups blanched almond flour

^{1}/$_2$ teaspoon sea salt

^{1}/$_2$ teaspoon baking soda

^{1}/$_4$ cup grapeseed oil

^{1}/$_4$ cup agave nectar

2 large eggs

1 teaspoon freshly squeezed lemon juice

Preheat the oven to 350°F. Line a large baking sheet with parchment paper.

In a large bowl, combine the almond flour, salt, and baking soda. In a medium bowl, whisk together the grapeseed oil, agave nectar, eggs, and lemon juice. Stir the wet ingredients into the almond flour mixture until thoroughly combined. Drop the batter, in scant ^{1}/4 cups 2 inches apart, onto the baking sheet.

Bake for 15 to 20 minutes, until golden brown or a toothpick inserted into the center of a biscuit comes out clean. Let the biscuits cool briefly on the baking sheet, then serve warm.

French Toast

I often make this French Toast for dinner on Sunday nights and serve it with turkey bacon or sausage. When it comes to toppings, the possibilities are endless—Cinnamon Apple Syrup (page 122) or Blueberry Sauce (page 122) are scrumptious, while Whipped Cream (page 126) is beyond decadent at dinnertime.

1/4 cup heavy cream or coconut milk

2 tablespoons agave nectar

4 large eggs

1 teaspoon vanilla extract

1/4 teaspoon sea salt

1/2 teaspoon ground cinnamon

8 (1/2-inch-thick) slices Scrumptious Sandwich Bread (page 26)

2 tablespoons grapeseed oil

In a medium bowl, whisk together the cream, agave nectar, eggs, vanilla extract, salt, and cinnamon until thoroughly combined. Pour the mixture into a 13 by 9-inch baking dish and soak the slices of bread in the mixture for 5 minutes on each side.

Heat the grapeseed oil in a large skillet over medium-high heat. Cook the bread slices in the oil for 3 to 5 minutes on each side, until golden brown. Transfer the French Toast to a plate.

Repeat the process with the remaining slices, then serve.

Pancakes

MAKES 12 PANCAKES ✦ SWEETNESS: LOW

These pancakes are a healthy, dairy-free, high-protein way to start the day. They offer something sweet for the morning that won't spike your blood sugar, especially when served with turkey bacon. Sprinkle berries or dark chocolate chips into the batter for a more creative take on breakfast. Make the batter in a blender to ensure the proper consistency.

2 large eggs   *1 egg white*

1/4 cup agave nectar

1 tablespoon vanilla extract

1/4 cup water   *2 T*

1 1/2 cups blanched almond flour   *3/4 C.*

1/2 teaspoon sea salt   *1/4 tsp*

1/2 teaspoon baking soda   *1/4 tsp*

1/4 tsp. Xanth gum 1 tablespoon arrowroot powder *1/8 tsp. Xanthan Gum*

(2 tablespoons grapeseed oil)

In a blender, combine the eggs, agave nectar, vanilla extract, and water; process on high for about 1 minute, until smooth. Add the almond flour, salt, baking soda, and arrowroot powder, and blend until thoroughly combined.

Heat the grapeseed oil in a large skillet over medium-low heat. Ladle 1 heaping tablespoon of the batter onto the skillet for each pancake. Cook until small bubbles form on the top of each pancake; when the bubbles begin to open, flip each pancake. When fully cooked, transfer the pancakes to a plate.

Repeat the process with the remaining batter, then serve.

Cinnamon Coffee Cake

SERVES 12 ✧ SWEETNESS: HIGH

Growing up, I was a huge fan of Sara Lee frozen coffee cakes, which were covered with a thick layer of supersweet white frosting and almond slices. My version of Sara Lee's best is inspired by Lucy Rosset of www.lucyskitchenshop.com. The cake's cinnamon topping and almond slices bring back childhood memories without the high sugar content and overly processed ingredients.

CAKE

2 1/2 cups blanched almond flour

1/4 teaspoon sea salt

1/2 teaspoon baking soda

1/2 cup walnuts, coarsely chopped

1/2 cup dried currants

1/4 cup grapeseed oil

1/4 cup agave nectar

2 large eggs

TOPPING

2 tablespoons ground cinnamon

2 tablespoons grapeseed oil

1/4 cup agave nectar

1/2 cup sliced almonds

Preheat the oven to 350°F. Grease an 8-inch square baking dish with grapeseed oil and dust with almond flour.

To make the cake, combine the almond flour, salt, baking soda, walnuts, and currants in a large bowl. In a medium bowl, whisk together the grapeseed oil, agave nectar, and eggs. Stir the wet ingredients into the almond flour mixture until thoroughly combined. Spread the batter in the baking dish.

To make the topping, combine the cinnamon, grapeseed oil, agave nectar, and almonds in a bowl. Sprinkle the topping over the cake batter.

Bake for 25 to 35 minutes, until a toothpick inserted into the center of the cake comes out clean. Let the cake cool in the pan for 1 hour, then serve.

Breads and Crackers

Scrumptious Sandwich Bread

MAKES 1 LOAF (ABOUT 12 SLICES)

One of the most challenging aspects of giving up gluten is finding good bread. This bread is easy to make since it has no yeast or rising time. It works well for sandwiches and French Toast (page 21). After it cools, wrap the bread in a paper towel, place in a resealable plastic bag, and refrigerate. Store all of the breads in this section this way and they will keep for up to six days, ready for your snack and sandwich needs.

- 3/4 cup creamy roasted almond butter, at room temperature
- 4 large eggs
- 1/4 cup blanched almond flour
- 1/4 cup arrowroot powder
- 1/2 teaspoon sea salt
- 1/2 teaspoon baking soda
- 1 tablespoon ground flax meal

Preheat the oven to 350°F. Grease a 7 by 3-inch loaf pan with grapeseed oil and dust with almond flour.

In a large bowl, mix the almond butter with a handheld mixer until smooth, then blend in the eggs. In a medium bowl, combine the almond flour, arrowroot powder, salt, baking soda, and flax meal. Blend the almond flour mixture into the wet ingredients until thoroughly combined. Pour the batter into the loaf pan.

Bake for 40 to 45 minutes on the bottom rack of the oven, until a knife inserted into the center of the loaf comes out clean. Let the bread cool in the pan for 1 hour, then serve.

Pecan-Raisin Bread

MAKES 1 LOAF (ABOUT 12 SLICES) ✦ SWEETNESS: LOW

When we lived in New York City, my husband and I were hooked on a particular pecan-raisin bread from the Upper West Side institution Zabar's. I am now very happy to have my own gluten-free version. I eat it plain, toasted, or spread with butter.

3/4 cup creamy roasted almond butter, at room temperature

4 large eggs

1/4 cup blanched almond flour

1/4 cup arrowroot powder

1/2 teaspoon sea salt

1/2 teaspoon baking soda

1 teaspoon ground cinnamon

1/2 cup pecans, coarsely chopped

1 cup raisins

Preheat the oven to 350°F. Grease a 7 by 3-inch loaf pan with grapeseed oil and dust with almond flour.

In a large bowl, mix the almond butter with a handheld mixer until smooth, and then blend in the eggs. In a medium bowl, combine the almond flour, arrowroot powder, salt, baking soda, and cinnamon. Blend the almond flour mixture into the wet ingredients until thoroughly combined, then fold in the pecans and raisins. Pour the batter into the loaf pan.

Bake for 45 to 50 minutes on the bottom rack of the oven, until a knife inserted into the center of the loaf comes out clean. Let the bread cool in the pan for 1 hour, then serve.

Muesli Bread

MAKES 1 LOAF (ABOUT 12 SLICES) ✢ SWEETNESS: LOW

I especially enjoy the food blog www.deliciousdays.com. Recently I saw a recipe for a wheat-based muesli bread on that site and used it as inspiration for this nutty, sweet fruit loaf. When I want a healthy treat after dinner, I toast a slice and spread it with goat cheese.

3/4 cup creamy roasted almond butter, at room temperature

1 tablespoon agave nectar

4 large eggs

1/4 cup blanched almond flour

1/4 cup arrowroot powder

1 teaspoon sea salt

1/2 teaspoon baking soda

1 teaspoon ground flax meal

1/4 cup dried apricots, chopped into 1/4-inch pieces

1/2 cup dried cranberries

1/2 cup pistachios, coarsely chopped

1/4 cup hazelnuts, coarsely chopped

1/4 cup sesame seeds

1/4 cup sunflower seeds

Preheat the oven to 350°F. Grease a 7 by 3-inch loaf pan with grapeseed oil and dust with almond flour.

In a large bowl, mix the almond butter and agave nectar with a handheld mixer until smooth, then blend in the eggs. In a medium bowl, combine the almond flour, arrowroot powder, salt, baking soda, and flax meal. Blend the almond flour mixture into the wet ingredients until thoroughly combined. Fold in the apricots, cranberries, pistachios, hazelnuts, sesame seeds, and sunflower seeds. Pour the batter into the loaf pan.

Bake for 50 to 60 minutes on the bottom rack of the oven, until a knife inserted into the center of the loaf comes out clean. Let the bread cool in the pan for 1 hour, then serve.

Olive-Rosemary Bread

MAKES 1 LOAF (ABOUT 12 SLICES)

To make a great base for hors d'oeuvres, cut this loaf into thin slices, spread on a baking sheet, and toast in the oven at 350°F for 5 to 10 minutes. The resulting crackers are great with goat cheese, drizzled with a good cold-pressed olive oil, or spread with fig tapenade (find the recipe on my blog).

3/4 cup creamy roasted almond butter, at room temperature

2 tablespoons olive oil

3 large eggs

1 tablespoon agave nectar

1/4 cup blanched almond flour

1/4 cup arrowroot powder

1/2 teaspoon sea salt

1/2 teaspoon baking soda

1/4 cup kalamata olives, pitted and finely chopped

1 tablespoon finely chopped fresh rosemary

Preheat the oven to 350°F. Grease a 7 by 3-inch loaf pan with grapeseed oil and dust with almond flour.

In a large bowl, mix the almond butter and olive oil with a handheld mixer until smooth, then blend in the eggs and agave nectar. In a medium bowl, combine the almond flour, arrowroot powder, salt, and baking soda. Blend the almond flour mixture into the wet ingredients until thoroughly combined, then fold in the olives and rosemary. Pour the batter into the loaf pan.

Bake for 45 to 55 minutes on the bottom rack of the oven, until a knife inserted into the center of the loaf comes out clean. Let the bread cool in the pan for 1 hour, then serve.

Zucchini Bread

MAKES 2 LOAVES (ABOUT 12 SLICES) ✣ SWEETNESS: MEDIUM

This is a great bread to make when the zucchini in your garden is about to be bitten by winter's first frost. You can make this recipe into child-friendly muffins by letting the little ones measure out the ingredients. Scoop the batter into paper-lined muffin tins and bake for 25 to 30 minutes.

2 cups blanched almond flour

1/2 teaspoon sea salt

1/2 teaspoon baking soda

1 teaspoon ground cinnamon

1/4 cup grapeseed oil

1/2 cup agave nectar

2 large eggs

1 cup grated zucchini

1/2 cup pecans, coarsely chopped

1/4 cup dried currants

Preheat the oven to 350°F. Grease 2 mini loaf pans with grapeseed oil and dust with almond flour.

In a large bowl, combine the almond flour, salt, baking soda, and cinnamon. In a medium bowl, whisk together the grapeseed oil, agave nectar, and eggs. Blend the almond flour mixture into the wet ingredients until thoroughly combined, then fold in the zucchini, pecans, and currants. Scoop the batter into the loaf pans.

Bake for 50 to 60 minutes on the bottom rack of the oven, until a knife inserted into the center of the loaf comes out clean. Let the bread cool in the pans for 1 hour, then serve.

Cheddar Cheese Crackers

Friends tell me these crackers taste like Cheez-Its, though with this healthy high-protein version, you don't have to worry about indulging. Forget about spreads and dips—these crackers are excellent on their own.

2 1/2 cups blanched almond flour
1/4 teaspoon sea salt
1/2 teaspoon baking soda
1 cup freshly grated Cheddar cheese
3 tablespoons grapeseed oil
2 large eggs

Preheat the oven to 350°F. Set aside 2 large baking sheets. Cut 3 pieces of parchment paper to the size of the baking sheets.

In a large bowl, combine the almond flour, salt, baking soda, and cheese. In a medium bowl, whisk together the grapeseed oil and eggs. Stir the wet ingredients into the almond flour mixture until thoroughly combined.

Divide the dough into 2 pieces. Place 1 piece of dough between 2 sheets of parchment paper and roll to 1/16-inch thickness. Remove the top piece of parchment paper and transfer the bottom piece of parchment with the rolled-out dough onto a baking sheet. Repeat the process with the remaining piece of dough. Cut the dough into 2-inch squares with a knife or pizza cutter.

Bake for 12 to 15 minutes, until lightly golden. Let the crackers cool on the baking sheets for 30 minutes, then serve.

Herb Crackers

MAKES 60 CRACKERS

A scrumptious scent fills the kitchen when these crackers are baking. They are delightful dipped in hummus, tahini, or baba ghanoush.

3½ cups blanched almond flour

1 teaspoon sea salt

2 tablespoons finely chopped fresh rosemary

2 tablespoons finely chopped fresh thyme

2 tablespoons grapeseed oil

2 large eggs

Preheat the oven to 350°F. Set aside 2 large baking sheets. Cut 3 pieces of parchment paper to the size of the baking sheets.

In a large bowl, combine the almond flour, salt, rosemary, and thyme. In a medium bowl, whisk together the grapeseed oil and eggs. Stir the wet ingredients into the almond flour mixture until thoroughly combined.

Divide the dough into 2 pieces. Place 1 piece of dough between 2 sheets of parchment paper and roll to $1/16$-inch thickness. Remove the top piece of parchment paper and transfer the bottom piece of parchment with the rolled-out dough onto a baking sheet. Repeat the process with the remaining piece of dough. Cut the dough into 2-inch squares with a knife or pizza cutter.

Bake for 12 to 15 minutes, until lightly golden. Let the crackers cool on the baking sheets for 30 minutes, then serve.

Pumpkin-Flax Crackers

MAKES 60 CRACKERS

These wholesome crackers full of omega 3–rich flax meal have a wonderfully crunchy texture and nutty flavor. Eat them plain, with lemon tahini, or a favorite dip of your own creation.

2 cups blanched almond flour

2 teaspoons sea salt

1 cup ground flax meal

1 cup sesame seeds

1 cup pumpkin seeds

1 tablespoon All Purpose Chef's Shake seasoning

3 tablespoons grapeseed oil

3 large eggs

Preheat the oven to 350°F. Set aside 2 large baking sheets. Cut 3 pieces of parchment paper to the size of the baking sheets.

In a large bowl, combine the almond flour, salt, flax meal, sesame seeds, pumpkin seeds, and Chef's Shake. In a medium bowl, whisk together the grapeseed oil and eggs. Stir the wet ingredients into the almond flour mixture until thoroughly combined.

Divide the dough into 2 pieces. Place 1 piece of dough between 2 sheets of parchment paper and roll to $1/8$-inch thickness. Remove the top piece of parchment paper and transfer the bottom piece of parchment with the rolled-out dough onto a baking sheet. Repeat the process with the remaining piece of dough. Cut the dough into 2-inch squares with a knife or pizza cutter.

Bake for 12 to 15 minutes, until lightly golden. Let the crackers cool on the baking sheets for 30 minutes, then serve.

Sesame Crackers

MAKES 60 CRACKERS

These sesame crackers are delicious plain; I eat them like chips, though with their high-protein content, sesame seeds, and distinct lack of deep frying, they are far healthier. They also make great dippers for guacamole.

3 cups blanched almond flour

1½ teaspoons sea salt

1 cup sesame seeds

2 tablespoons grapeseed oil

2 large eggs

Preheat the oven to 350°F. Set aside 2 large baking sheets. Cut 3 pieces of parchment paper to the size of the baking sheets.

In a large bowl, combine the almond flour, salt, and sesame seeds. In a medium bowl, whisk together the grapeseed oil and eggs. Stir the wet ingredients into the almond flour mixture until thoroughly combined.

Divide the dough into 2 pieces. Place 1 piece of dough between 2 sheets of parchment paper and roll to $1/16$-inch thickness. Remove the top piece of parchment paper and transfer the bottom piece of parchment with the rolled-out dough onto a baking sheet. Repeat the process with the remaining piece of dough. Cut the dough into 2-inch squares with a knife or pizza cutter.

Bake for 12 to 15 minutes, until lightly golden. Let the crackers cool on the baking sheets for 30 minutes, then serve.

Spicy Crackers

MAKES 60 CRACKERS

These zesty crackers have a Middle-Eastern flair and are very versatile; you can eat them plain, dipped in tahini, or spread with cream cheese. The cumin in this cracker provides more than great flavor—this immune-boosting spice is high in iron as well.

3 cups blanched almond flour

1½ teaspoons sea salt

½ cup pecans, coarsely chopped

1 tablespoon ground smoked paprika

½ teaspoon ground cumin

2 tablespoons grapeseed oil

2 large eggs

1 teaspoon lemon zest

Preheat the oven to 350°F. Set aside 2 large baking sheets. Cut 3 pieces of parchment paper to the size of the baking sheets.

In a large bowl, combine the almond flour, salt, pecans, paprika, and cumin. In a medium bowl, whisk together the grapeseed oil, eggs, and lemon zest. Stir the wet ingredients into the almond flour mixture until thoroughly combined.

Divide the dough into 2 pieces. Place 1 piece of dough between 2 sheets of parchment paper and roll to ¹/₁₆-inch thickness. Remove the top piece of parchment paper and transfer the bottom piece of parchment with the rolled-out dough onto a baking sheet. Repeat the process with the remaining piece of dough. Cut the dough into 2-inch squares with a knife or pizza cutter.

Bake for 12 to 15 minutes, until lightly golden. Let the crackers cool on the baking sheets for 30 minutes, then serve.

Entrées

Chicken Fingers

SERVES 4

My boys love chicken fingers dipped in ketchup. For adults, I serve this dish with a homemade orange-ginger sauce. For leftovers, cut up the strips and serve with a Thai peanut sauce over steamed broccoli and clear mung bean noodles, which can be found at most Asian markets.

1 pound boneless, skinless chicken breasts

1 cup blanched almond flour

1 teaspoon sea salt

2 large eggs

2 tablespoons grapeseed oil

2 tablespoons olive oil

Rinse the chicken, pat dry, and slice into 2-inch-wide strips.

In a medium bowl, combine the almond flour and salt. In a separate bowl, whisk the eggs. Dip each chicken strip into the egg, then coat with the almond flour mixture.

Heat the grapeseed and olive oils in a large skillet over medium-high heat. Sauté the chicken in the oil for 3 to 6 minutes per side, until golden brown.

Transfer the chicken to a paper towel–lined plate and serve hot.

Chicken Parmesan

SERVES 4

Each year I serve this Chicken Parmesan for my husband's birthday. Tender, moist chicken, piquantly seasoned sauce, and creamy melted cheese combine to create the ideal make-ahead dinner choice for any special occasion. You can prepare this entrée the night before you intend to serve it, if you cook the chicken, layer it with the cheese and sauce in the dish, and refrigerate it. Bake the chicken, and in mere minutes wow your guests with this classic Italian dish.

2 to 4 boneless, skinless chicken breast halves (about 1^1/$_2$ pounds)

1^1/$_2$ cups blanched almond flour

1 teaspoon sea salt

2 large eggs

2 tablespoons grapeseed oil

2 tablespoons olive oil

2 cups Tomato Sauce (page 123)

2 cups freshly grated mozzarella cheese

^{1}/$_4$ cup freshly grated Parmesan cheese

❖

Preheat the oven to 350°F.

Rinse the chicken and pat dry. Cut the chicken breast halves horizontally, butter-flying them open, then pound each with a skillet to flatten. Cut each breast half into 2 pieces.

In a medium bowl, combine the almond flour and salt. In a separate bowl, whisk the eggs. Dip each cutlet into the egg, then coat with the almond flour mixture.

Heat the grapeseed and olive oils in a large skillet over medium high-heat. Sauté the chicken in the oil for 3 to 5 minutes per side, until golden brown. Transfer the chicken to a paper towel–lined plate.

Pour 1 cup of the Tomato Sauce into a 13 by 9-inch baking dish. Place the cutlets in a single layer over the sauce. Cover the chicken with the remaining sauce, then top with the mozzarella.

Bake for 10 to 15 minutes, until the cheese is melted and the edges are bubbling. Remove from the oven and top with grated Parmesan before serving.

Chicken Piccata

SERVES 4

Elise of www.simplyrecipes.com is one of my favorite food bloggers. I adapted her version of this dish to fit my dietary needs by removing the wine, wheat, and butter.

4 boneless, skinless chicken breast halves (about 1½ pounds)

½ cup blanched almond flour

½ teaspoon sea salt

½ teaspoon All Purpose Chef's Shake seasoning

2 tablespoons olive oil

5 tablespoons grapeseed oil

¼ cup freshly squeezed lemon juice

1 cup chicken stock

¼ cup capers

¼ cup finely chopped fresh parsley

Rinse the chicken and pat dry. Cut the chicken breast halves horizontally, butterflying them open, then pound each with a skillet to flatten.

In a medium bowl, combine the almond flour, salt, and Chef's Shake. Coat the chicken with the almond flour mixture.

Heat the olive oil and 2 tablespoons of the grapeseed oil in a large skillet over medium-high heat. Sauté the chicken in the oil for 3 to 5 minutes per side, until golden brown. Transfer the chicken to a paper towel–lined plate and place in a warm oven.

Using the same skillet, combine the lemon juice, chicken stock, and capers, loosening the browned bits with a spatula to incorporate into the sauce. Reduce the sauce by half over medium-high heat. Whisk in the remaining 3 tablespoons grapeseed oil.

Pour the sauce over the chicken and sprinkle with parsley before serving.

Chicken Pot Pie

SERVES 6

On a cold day, there is nothing more comforting than homemade chicken pot pie. This quick and easy Chicken Pot Pie does not require any baking—make your filling on the stovetop, pour it into the pre-baked crust, and this dish is ready to serve.

1 pound boneless, skinless chicken breasts
2 tablespoons grapeseed oil
1 large onion, finely chopped
2 stalks celery, diced into $1/4$-inch cubes
2 medium carrots, diced into $1/4$-inch cubes
1 teaspoon sea salt
1 cup thinly sliced mushrooms
$1/2$ cup finely chopped fresh parsley
$1/2$ cup frozen peas
2 tablespoons arrowroot powder
1 cup chicken stock
1 Savory Pie Crust (page 81), prebaked
Pinch of freshly ground black pepper

Rinse the chicken and pat dry. Cut the chicken into $1/2$-inch cubes, transfer to a plate, and refrigerate.

Heat the grapeseed oil in a large skillet over medium-high heat. Sauté the onion for 8 to 10 minutes, until soft, then decrease the heat to medium. Add the celery, carrots, and salt; cook covered for 10 to 15 minutes, until tender. Stir in the mushrooms and chicken, and cook covered for 3 to 5 minutes, until the chicken is cooked through. Stir in the parsley and peas.

In a small bowl, vigorously whisk the arrowroot powder into the chicken stock until dissolved. Raise the heat under the chicken-vegetable mixture to high, then add the arrowroot mixture, whisking constantly for about 1 minute, until thick.

Pour the mixture into the crust, top with pepper, and serve hot.

Pistachio Chicken

SERVES 4

This quick and easy recipe requires minimal preparation and yields maximum results. The unique and tangy combination of pistachios and mustard is equally suited to a festive dinner or a casual picnic. I often bring this dish to potlucks to offer a healthy, high-quality protein that is appealing to adults and children alike.

1 1/2 pounds boneless, skinless chicken breasts

2 tablespoons blanched almond flour

1/4 cup arrowroot powder

1 teaspoon sea salt

2 large eggs

1 tablespoon grapeseed oil

1 tablespoon olive oil

1/4 cup Dijon mustard

2 1/4 cups pistachios, toasted and finely chopped

Preheat the oven to 425°F. Generously grease a large baking sheet with grapeseed oil.

Rinse the chicken, pat dry, and slice into 1/2-inch-wide strips.

In a medium bowl, combine the almond flour, arrowroot powder, and salt. In a separate bowl, whisk together the eggs, grapeseed oil, olive oil, and mustard. Place the pistachios in a separate bowl.

Coat the chicken strips first in the flour mixture, then in the egg mixture, and finally in the pistachios. Place on the prepared baking sheet.

Bake for 10 minutes, or until the pistachios are golden brown and the chicken is cooked through. Serve hot.

Matzo Ball Soup

SERVES 6

Traditionally served in a chicken stock during Passover or on the Sabbath, matzo balls are an Eastern European Jewish dish made from wheat-based matzo meal. These nourishing, high-protein, almond-based matzo balls are the perfect comfort food on any wintry day.

4 large eggs

2 teaspoons sea salt

$1/4$ teaspoon freshly ground black pepper

2 cups blanched almond flour

6 cups chicken stock

✥

In a medium bowl, whisk the eggs, 1 teaspoon of the salt, and the pepper with a handheld mixer for 2 to 3 minutes, until fluffy. Stir in the almond flour and refrigerate the mixture for about 3 hours, until firm.

Fill a stockpot with water and bring to a boil. While waiting for the water to boil, scoop 1 heaping teaspoon of the matzo-ball mixture into the palm of your hand and roll into a $1^1/2$-inch ball. Repeat the process until all of the batter is formed into balls and reserve to a plate. When the water is boiling, add the remaining 1 teaspoon salt. Drop the matzo balls into the boiling water. Decrease the heat, cover, and simmer for 20 minutes.

In a separate large pot, heat the chicken stock to a gentle simmer. Remove the matzo balls from the water with a slotted spoon and add to the chicken stock.

Ladle 2 to 3 matzo balls and chicken stock into individual bowls and serve piping hot.

Turkey Burgers

SERVES 4

These are my take on Oprah's favorite "Mar-a-Lago Burger," with the standard green apple, though I have added a hefty dose of Dijon mustard to give them extra zing. To make a light and healthy "bun," wrap the burger in a piece of romaine lettuce and smother with your favorite condiments.

5 tablespoons grapeseed oil

1/4 cup thinly sliced scallions (white and green parts)

1/4 cup finely chopped celery

1 medium Granny Smith apple, peeled, cored, and diced into 1/4-inch cubes

1 pound ground turkey

1/4 cup finely chopped fresh parsley

2 tablespoons Dijon mustard

1 tablespoon freshly squeezed lemon juice

1 teaspoon lemon zest

1 large egg

1/2 cup blanched almond flour

1 teaspoon sea salt

1 teaspoon freshly ground black pepper

Heat 2 tablespoons of the grapeseed oil in a large skillet over medium heat. Sauté the scallions, celery, and apple for 5 to 10 minutes, until tender; remove from the heat and let cool.

In a large bowl, combine the ground turkey and the sautéed ingredients. Mix in 1 tablespoon of the grapeseed oil, the parsley, mustard, lemon juice, lemon zest, egg, almond flour, salt, and pepper. Form the mixture into 2-inch patties.

Heat the remaining grapeseed oil in a large skillet over medium-high heat. Cook the patties for 4 to 6 minutes per side, until golden brown. Transfer the patties to a paper towel–lined plate and serve hot.

Herbed Turkey Loaf

SERVES 4

Meat loaf was the main course at my father's birthday dinner every year before he gave up red meat. I had him in mind when I created this lower-cholesterol version with ground turkey in place of beef.

1 pound ground turkey

1 tablespoon grapeseed oil

1 medium onion, finely chopped

1 clove garlic, minced

1/2 cup shredded zucchini

2 large eggs, whisked

1/4 cup ketchup

1/2 cup blanched almond flour

1 teaspoon sea salt

1/2 teaspoon freshly ground black pepper

1/4 cup finely chopped fresh parsley

1 tablespoon minced fresh thyme

Preheat the oven to 350°F. Line a large baking sheet with parchment paper.

In a large bowl, combine the turkey, grapeseed oil, onion, garlic, zucchini, eggs, and ketchup. In a medium bowl, combine the almond flour, salt, pepper, parsley, and thyme. Stir the almond flour mixture into the wet ingredients, then knead with your hands until well combined. Form the mixture into a loaf approximately 10 inches long by 3 inches wide and place on the prepared baking sheet.

Bake for 50 to 60 minutes, until browned around the edges and cooked through. Remove the loaf from the oven and allow to sit for 5 to 10 minutes. Slice and serve.

Fish Sticks

SERVES 4

These Fish Sticks receive a warm reception from children when served with ketchup. If you wish to prepare a more elegant dish, serve them over a bed of fresh mixed salad greens or with steamed broccoli and a ginger-orange dressing.

$1^1/_2$ pounds cod fillet

$1^1/_2$ cups blanched almond flour

1 teaspoon sea salt

2 large eggs

2 tablespoons grapeseed oil

2 tablespoons olive oil

Rinse the cod, pat dry, and slice into $1^1/_2$-inch-wide strips.

In a medium bowl, combine the almond flour and salt. In a separate bowl, whisk the eggs. Dip each cod strip into the egg, then coat with the almond flour mixture.

Heat the grapeseed and olive oils in a large skillet over medium-high heat. Sauté the cod in the oil for 3 to 5 minutes per side, until golden brown.

Transfer the cod to a paper towel–lined plate and serve.

Cod Piccata Paprika

SERVES 4

This recipe is a twist on the classic lemon-and-caper-based Italian piccata sauce. Here I feature spicy smoked paprika and tangy kalamata olives, creating a unique, savory flavor. I've used cod, though halibut would also work well. The trick is to choose a thicker fish that can absorb this spicy sauce. Serve with a big green salad or steamed kale.

1 1/2 pounds cod fillet
1/2 cup blanched almond flour
1/2 teaspoon sea salt
1/4 teaspoon ground smoked paprika
2 tablespoons olive oil
4 tablespoons grapeseed oil
1 cup chicken stock
1/4 cup freshly squeezed lemon juice
1/4 cup kalamata olives, finely chopped
1/4 cup finely chopped fresh parsley

Rinse the cod, pat dry, and slice into 4 pieces.

In a medium bowl, combine the almond flour, salt, and paprika. Coat the cod with the almond flour mixture.

Heat the olive oil and 1 tablespoon of the grapeseed oil in a large skillet over medium-high heat. Sauté the cod in the oil for 3 to 5 minutes per side, until golden brown. Transfer the cod to a paper towel–lined plate and place in a warm oven.

Using the same skillet, combine the chicken stock, lemon juice, and olives, loosening the browned bits with a spatula to incorporate into the sauce. Raise the heat to high and reduce the sauce by half. Whisk in the remaining 3 tablespoons grapeseed oil.

Pour the sauce over the cod, and sprinkle with parsley before serving.

Salmon Dill Burgers

SERVES 4

These burgers are a favorite dish among fish-phobic friends and family. The refreshing lemon and dill flavors give the salmon a light and subtle role in this satisfying burger.

1 pound skinless salmon fillet

1/2 cup blanched almond flour

2 large eggs

1 tablespoon lemon zest

1 tablespoon finely chopped fresh dill

1/2 teaspoon sea salt

2 tablespoons grapeseed oil

Rinse the salmon, pat dry, and cut into 1/4-inch cubes.

In a large bowl, combine the salmon, almond flour, eggs, lemon zest, dill, and salt. Form the mixture into 2-inch patties.

Heat the grapeseed oil in a large skillet over medium-high heat. Cook the patties 4 to 6 minutes per side, until golden brown. Transfer the patties to a paper towel–lined plate and serve.

Smoked Salmon–Leek Tart

SERVES 6

Topped with goat cheese, this tart is an excellent replacement for the classic bagel and lox. Be sure to use scallions in the Herb Tart Crust as a complement to the salmon and leek.

2 tablespoons grapeseed oil

2 cups thinly sliced leeks (white and green parts)

2 ounces smoked salmon, coarsely chopped

1 tablespoon finely chopped fresh dill

1/2 teaspoon sea salt

4 large eggs, whisked

1 Herb Tart Crust (page 82), prebaked

Preheat the oven to 350°F.

Heat the grapeseed oil in a large skillet over medium heat. Sauté the leeks for 10 to 15 minutes, until lightly browned. In a large bowl, combine the leeks, smoked salmon, dill, salt, and eggs. Pour the mixture into the crust.

Bake for 25 to 30 minutes, until browned around the edges and cooked through. Let the tart cool in the pan for 30 minutes, then serve.

Southwestern Salmon Burgers

SERVES 4

A colorful blend of bright red peppers, fresh citrus, cilantro, and a spicy dash of chipotle, these tasty burgers, packed with omega-3s, make a frequent appearance on our dinner table.

1 pound skinless salmon fillet

3/4 cup blanched almond flour

2 large eggs

1 red bell pepper, diced into 1/4-inch cubes

1 tablespoon minced fresh cilantro

1 tablespoon finely chopped scallions (white and green parts)

1 teaspoon sea salt

1 teaspoon ground cumin

1 teaspoon ground chipotle

1 tablespoon freshly squeezed lime juice

2 tablespoons grapeseed oil

Rinse the salmon, pat dry, and cut into 1/4-inch cubes.

In a large bowl, combine the salmon, almond flour, eggs, bell pepper, cilantro, scallions, salt, cumin, chipotle, and lime juice. Form the mixture into 2-inch patties.

Heat the grapeseed oil in a large skillet over medium-high heat. Cook the patties for 4 to 6 minutes per side, until golden brown. Transfer the patties to a paper towel–lined plate and serve hot.

Thai Fish Cakes

SERVES 4

The coconut and lime in these unique fish cakes lend an Asian flavor to this high-protein dish. For your next cocktail party, form them into little balls, sauté, and serve with a peanut dipping sauce—your hungry guests will enjoy the unique blend of flavors in this spectacular hors d'oeuvre.

1 pound skinless snapper fillet

1/4 cup blanched almond flour

1/2 cup unsweetened shredded coconut, toasted

3 large eggs

1 tablespoon minced fresh cilantro

1 tablespoon peeled and minced fresh ginger

1 tablespoon finely chopped scallions (white and green parts)

1/2 teaspoon sea salt

1 tablespoon fish sauce

1 tablespoon lime zest

2 tablespoons grapeseed oil

Rinse the snapper, pat dry, and cut into 1/4-inch cubes.

In a large bowl, combine the snapper, almond flour, coconut, eggs, cilantro, ginger, scallions, salt, fish sauce, and lime zest. Form the mixture into 2-inch patties.

Heat the grapeseed oil in a large skillet over medium-high heat. Cook the patties for 4 to 6 minutes per side, until golden brown. Transfer the patties to a paper towel–lined plate and serve.

Shrimp Fritters

These fritters, adapted from a recipe by Amanda Hesser, are full of delicate Thai flavors. I often serve them wrapped in leaves of Boston or Romaine lettuce and sprinkled with nuoc mam, a Vietnamese fish sauce.

1 pound raw shrimp, peeled and deveined, tails removed

$1/2$ cup blanched almond flour

$1/4$ cup thinly sliced scallions (white and green parts)

1 tablespoon finely chopped fresh cilantro

1 tablespoon finely chopped fresh mint leaves

1 tablespoon peeled and minced fresh ginger

$1/4$ teaspoon ground paprika

$1/4$ teaspoon sea salt

1 tablespoon fish sauce

1 tablespoon toasted sesame oil

1 tablespoon agave nectar

2 large eggs

2 tablespoons grapeseed oil

2 limes, for garnish

Rinse the shrimp, pat dry, and cut into $1/4$-inch pieces.

Place the shrimp pieces in a food processor and pulse until well chopped. In a large bowl, combine the shrimp, almond flour, scallions, cilantro, mint, ginger, paprika, salt, fish sauce, sesame oil, agave nectar, and eggs. Refrigerate the mixture for 30 minutes, then form into 2-inch patties.

Heat the grapeseed oil in a large skillet over medium-high heat. Cook the patties for 4 to 6 minutes per side, until golden brown. Transfer the patties to a paper towel–lined plate. Garnish with lime wedges and serve.

Black Bean Burgers

SERVES 6

Healthy and flavorful, these burgers make a great vegetarian entrée served with sliced avocado or a hearty breakfast with a side of spicy scrambled eggs and salsa. Beans are a cost-effective source of protein, especially when purchased in bulk rather than in cans.

3 tablespoons grapeseed oil

1 medium onion, coarsely chopped

5 cloves garlic, thinly sliced

1 medium red bell pepper, diced into 1/4-inch cubes

2 cups black beans, cooked

2 teaspoons sea salt

1 tablespoon ground cumin

1 teaspoon ground chipotle

1/4 cup minced fresh cilantro

3 large eggs

1/2 cup blanched almond flour

Heat 1 tablespoon of the grapeseed oil in a large skillet over medium heat. Sauté the onion for 8 to 10 minutes, until soft and translucent. Add the garlic and bell pepper, and sauté for 2 to 3 minutes, until softened.

In a large bowl, combine the onion mixture, beans, salt, cumin, chipotle, cilantro, eggs, and almond flour. Form the mixture into 2-inch patties.

Heat the remaining 2 tablespoons of grapeseed oil in a large skillet over medium-high heat. Cook the patties for 4 to 6 minutes per side, until browned around the edges. Transfer the patties to a paper towel–lined plate and serve.

Broccoli Pizza

SERVES 4

Pizza day comes once a week at my children's school. I often make it for dinner the night before and then send some with the boys for lunch the next day so that they can partake in the school pizza ritual— albeit in a gluten-free, organic way.

1 cup Pizza Sauce (page 123)
1 Pizza Crust (page 82), prebaked
1/2 cup freshly grated Cheddar cheese
1/2 cup freshly grated mozzarella cheese
4 cups broccoli, steamed

Preheat the oven to 350°F.

Spread the Pizza Sauce over the crust. Distribute the cheeses evenly over the sauce and top with the broccoli.

Bake for 10 to 15 minutes, until the cheese is melted. Let the pizza cool briefly before serving.

Eggplant Parmesan

SERVES 4

This is one of those remarkable dishes that magically tastes even better the next day. Over time, the eggplant soaks up additional flavor making it that much more appetizing. Less complex than the traditional version, you'll find my recipe easier to make as I've eliminated the time-consuming steps of peeling and salting the eggplant.

1½ pounds eggplant

1½ cups blanched almond flour

1 teaspoon sea salt

2 large eggs

2 tablespoons water

2 tablespoons grapeseed oil

2 tablespoons olive oil

3 cups Tomato Sauce (page 123)

2 cups freshly grated mozzarella cheese

¼ cup freshly grated Parmesan cheese

⊹

Preheat the oven to 350°F.

Cut the eggplant into ¼-inch slices. In a medium bowl, combine the almond flour and salt. In a separate bowl, whisk together the eggs and water. Dip the eggplant slices in the egg mixture, then coat with the almond flour mixture.

Heat the grapeseed and olive oils in a large skillet over medium-high heat. Sauté the eggplant for 3 to 5 minutes per side, until golden brown. Transfer the eggplant to a paper towel–lined plate.

Pour 1 cup of the Tomato Sauce into a 13 by 9-inch baking dish. Layer the eggplant over the sauce; cover the eggplant with 1 cup of the sauce and 1 cup of the mozzarella. Place the remaining eggplant over the top, then cover with the remaining sauce and mozzarella.

Bake for 10 to 15 minutes, until the cheese is melted and the edges are bubbling. Remove from the oven and top with grated Parmesan cheese before serving.

Savory Vegetable Quiche

SERVES 6

This easy quiche is versatile enough for breakfast, lunch, or dinner.
It's filled with three nutritious vegetables that are rich in antioxidants—
broccoli, tomatoes, and mushrooms—though it's so tasty that you
won't stop to think about the hefty dose of vitamins in every bite!

2 tablespoons grapeseed oil

1 medium onion, thinly sliced

2 cups broccoli, sliced into small spears
(about 1 head broccoli)

1 clove garlic, thinly sliced

1 cup thinly sliced mushrooms

1/4 cup finely chopped sun-dried tomatoes
(dry packed)

3 large eggs, whisked

4 ounces goat cheese

1/2 teaspoon sea salt

1 Savory Pie Crust (page 81), prebaked

Preheat the oven to 350°F.

Heat the grapeseed oil in a large skillet over medium heat. Sauté the onion for 8 to 10 minutes, until soft and translucent. While the onion is sautéing, steam the broccoli until it is bright green. Add the steamed broccoli, garlic, mushrooms, and tomatoes to the onion, and sauté for 15 to 20 minutes, until the broccoli softens. In a large bowl, combine the eggs, cheese, and salt. Stir in the sautéed vegetables, then pour the mixture into the crust.

Bake for 30 to 35 minutes, until browned around the edges and cooked through. Let the quiche cool in the pan for 30 minutes, then serve.

Asparagus Onion Quiche

SERVES 6

Rich in vitamin C, vitamin K, and folate, asparagus is one of the most nutritious vegetables around. Celebrate asparagus season (mid-April through mid-June) with this luscious quiche recipe. It's simple to prepare and a delight for dinner. Also delectable cold, it can be the star of your next picnic.

2 tablespoons grapeseed oil

2 medium red onions, thinly sliced

4 cups asparagus, cut into 1/4-inch slices

1 clove garlic, thinly sliced

3 large eggs, whisked

1 1/2 cups freshly grated Cheddar cheese

1/2 teaspoon sea salt

1 tablespoon finely chopped fresh basil

1 Savory Pie Crust (page 81), prebaked

Preheat the oven to 350°F.

Heat the grapeseed oil in a large skillet over medium heat. Sauté the onions for 8 to 10 minutes, until soft and translucent. While the onions are sautéing, steam the asparagus until it is bright green. Add the steamed asparagus along with the garlic to the onion, and sauté for 10 to 12 minutes, until the asparagus is almost tender.

In a large bowl, combine the eggs, cheese, salt, and basil. Stir in the sautéed vegetables, then pour the mixture into the crust.

Bake for 30 to 35 minutes, until browned around the edges and cooked through. Let the quiche cool in the pan for 30 minutes, then serve.

Kale Tart with Cranberries

SERVES 6

I use rosemary in the crust of this vegetable tart as the sharpness of this herb complements the earthy taste of kale. Deep green and flecked with bright cranberries, this dish is a colorful taste of autumn and a wonderful vegetarian addition to any Thanksgiving feast.

3 cups coarsely chopped kale

1 tablespoon thinly sliced shallots

1/2 teaspoon sea salt

3 large eggs, whisked

1/4 cup dried cranberries

1/4 cup pine nuts

1 Herb Tart Crust (page 82), prebaked

Preheat the oven to 350°F.

In a large pot with a steamer basket, wilt the kale over medium heat for 2 to 3 minutes, until bright green.

Place the kale, shallots, and salt in a food processor and pulse until well-blended. Transfer the kale mixture to a bowl and stir in the eggs, cranberries, and pine nuts. Pour the mixture into the crust.

Bake for 15 to 20 minutes, until browned around the edges and cooked through. Let the tart cool in the pan for 30 minutes, then serve.

Spinach Sun-Dried Tomato Tart

SERVES 6

Spinach and sun-dried tomatoes are a classic culinary combination brimming with health-building vitamin C, carotenoids, and iron. Crumble goat cheese over the top of this tart for a delightful finishing touch.

2 tablespoons grapeseed oil

3 medium shallots, thinly sliced

1 pound baby spinach

1/4 cup finely chopped sun-dried tomatoes (dry packed)

3 large eggs, whisked

1 Herb Tart Crust (page 82), prebaked

Preheat the oven to 350°F.

Heat the grapeseed oil in a large skillet over medium heat. Sauté the shallots for 8 to 10 minutes, until lightly browned. Add the spinach and sun-dried tomatoes, cover the pan, and cook for about 5 minutes, until the spinach wilts.

In a large bowl, combine the spinach mixture and eggs. Pour the mixture into the crust. Bake for 30 to 35 minutes, until browned around the edges and cooked through. Let the tart cool in the pan for 30 minutes, then serve.

Pies, Pastries, and Crusts

Skillet Apple Pie

SERVES 8 ✦ SWEETNESS: MEDIUM

This no-fuss apple pie tastes even better than its traditional cousin. Because the apples are caramelized before baking, it requires far less cooking time—only 20 minutes. My dairy-free, naturally sweetened version is based on an article in *Cook's Illustrated* called "Rethinking Apple Pie" by Yvonne Ruperti. Make this pie with any type of crunchy red apple, or for a tart twist, use Granny Smith.

CRUST

1 cup blanched almond flour

1 tablespoon arrowroot powder

1/2 teaspoon sea salt

2 tablespoons grapeseed oil

1 tablespoon agave nectar

FILLING

2 tablespoons grapeseed oil

5 medium apples (about 2 1/2 pounds), peeled, cored, and sliced 1/4 inch thick

1/2 cup apple juice

1/4 cup agave nectar

2 tablespoons freshly squeezed lemon juice

1 tablespoon arrowroot powder

1/2 teaspoon ground cinnamon

EGG WASH

1 egg white

Position an oven rack in the upper part of the oven. Preheat the oven to 500°F.

To make the crust, blend together the almond flour, arrowroot powder, and salt in a food processor. Pulse in the grapeseed oil and agave nectar. Blend until the mixture is crumbly, about 10 seconds. Transfer the dough to a bowl and place in the freezer for 20 minutes.

To make the filling, heat the grapeseed oil in a 12-inch skillet over medium-high heat. Sauté the apples, stirring occasionally until lightly caramelized, about 5 minutes. Remove from the heat.

In a medium bowl, whisk the apple juice, agave nectar, lemon juice, arrowroot powder, and cinnamon. Stir the apple juice mixture into the skillet with the caramelized apples.

Remove the dough from the freezer and form into a ball. Place the dough between 2 sheets of parchment paper generously dusted with almond flour, and roll the dough into an 11-inch circle, $^1/_{16}$ inch thick. Remove the top sheet of parchment and place the circle of dough over the skillet filled with caramelized apples. Peel back the remaining sheet of parchment paper and allow the dough to gently fall onto the apples. (The dough will crumble and break a bit—this is normal.) In a small bowl, whisk the egg white, then brush it over the crust.

Bake for 5 to 7 minutes, checking frequently, until golden brown. Turn the oven off. Carefully move the pie to a lower oven rack and leave in for an additional 5 to 10 minutes, until the crust is a deep golden, almost dark brown.

Serve the pie hot out of the oven.

Pecan Pie

SERVES 8 ✦ SWEETNESS: HIGH

Brimming with fragrant toasted pecans, this sumptuous Pecan Pie is a classic, though mine is a lot less sweet than the traditional version. Create culinary harmony by using my Dark Chocolate Pie Crust (page 79) as a base and topping with Whipped Cream (page 126). When making the filling, the trick is to cook the agar flakes at a high temperature so that they thoroughly dissolve.

1¹/₂ cups water

2 tablespoons agar flakes *or 1 ⅛ tsp pow-der*

¹/₂ teaspoon sea salt

1¹/₂ cups agave nectar *xylitol syrup*

1 tablespoon vanilla extract

1 teaspoon ground cinnamon

3 cups whole pecans, toasted

1 Dark Chocolate Pie Crust (page 79), prebaked

In a medium saucepan, bring the water to a boil, add the agar flakes, and cook over high heat, stirring frequently, until the agar flakes dissolve, 10 to 12 minutes. Decrease the heat and whisk in the salt, agave nectar, vanilla extract, and cinnamon. Continue cooking over medium heat for 2 to 3 minutes, stirring frequently until all ingredients are well incorporated.

Allow the mixture to cool to room temperature, and stir in the pecans.

Pour the mixture into the cooled pie crust and refrigerate for 1 hour, or until the pie has set. Serve.

Pumpkin Pie

SERVES 8 ✧ SWEETNESS: MEDIUM

My younger son devours this Thanksgiving staple every year. Our guests are not surprised to find that I make a gluten-free pumpkin pie, however, the ones that don't eat dairy are thrilled to find a version that has no milk or cream in it. For a detailed tutorial on pumpkin preparation from scratch, visit my blog.

3 to 4 pounds small pie pumpkin, acorn, or butternut squash

1 tablespoon ground cinnamon

1 teaspoon ground nutmeg

1/4 teaspoon ground ginger

Pinch of ground cloves

1/2 teaspoon sea salt

3/4 cup agave nectar

2 large eggs

1 tablespoon vanilla extract

1 tablespoon freshly squeezed lemon juice

1 Pie Crust (page 79), prebaked

Preheat the oven to 350°F.

Fill the bottom of a baking dish with 1/4 inch of water. Cut the pumpkin in half, remove the seeds, and place face down in the baking dish. Roast the pumpkin in the oven for 45 to 55 minutes, until soft. Allow the pumpkin to cool, scrape the flesh into a bowl, then measure out 4 cups.

Puree the pumpkin in a food processor until smooth, 2 to 3 minutes. Add the cinnamon, nutmeg, ginger, cloves, salt, agave nectar, eggs, vanilla extract, and lemon juice. Pulse until well blended. Pour the mixture into the crust.

Bake for 50 to 60 minutes, until the filling is firm. Let the pie cool in the pan for 30 minutes, then serve warm.

Chocolate Cream Pie

SERVES 8 ✦ SWEETNESS: HIGH

Be sure to let the coconut mixture cool before adding the chocolate
so that the filling for this pie does not take on a scorched flavor. I use
organic dark chocolate in this recipe because, unlike milk chocolate,
it is high in antioxidants.

28 ounces unsweetened coconut milk

Pinch of sea salt

1/4 cup arrowroot powder

1/2 cup agave nectar —xylitol syrup

2 tablespoons vanilla extract

2 cups coarsely chopped dark chocolate
(73% cacao) — 1 cup cacao paste

1 Pie Crust (page 79), prebaked

1/4 c Irish moss
    took alot more sweetner—

    1/2 c. xylitol
    1/2 tsp stevia

Reserve 1/4 cup of the coconut milk. In a medium saucepan, bring the remaining coconut milk and the salt to a boil; whisk constantly for 1 minute, then decrease to a simmer.

In a small bowl, dissolve the arrowroot powder in the reserved coconut milk, stirring to make a paste. Raise the heat under the saucepan to high and add the arrowroot paste to the saucepan, whisking constantly until the mixture thickens, about 1 minute. Stir in the agave nectar and vanilla extract.

Remove from the heat and allow to cool for 5 minutes. Add the chocolate to the coconut-arrowroot mixture, stirring vigorously until it is completely melted. Let the filling cool, then pour the mixture into the crust. Place in the refrigerator for 1 hour to set, then serve.

Peach Blueberry Crumble

SERVES 8 ❖ SWEETNESS: LOW

For a purely fruit-sweetened treat, try this flavorful crumble. Tasty, wholesome, and perfect with fresh summer fruit, it is ideal for breakfast with a cup of tea or for dessert with a dollop of Whipped Cream (page 126).

FILLING

4 fresh peaches, peeled and sliced, or 3 cups frozen peach slices, thawed

1 cup fresh or frozen blueberries, thawed

¼ c Xylitol

TOPPING

2 cups blanched almond flour

¹/₂ teaspoon sea salt

1 teaspoon ground cinnamon

¹/₂ teaspoon ground nutmeg

¹/₄ cup grapeseed oil

1 tablespoon vanilla extract

Preheat the oven to 350°F.

To make the filling, place the peaches and blueberries in an 8-inch baking dish.

To make the topping, combine the almond flour, salt, cinnamon, and nutmeg in a large bowl. In a medium bowl, whisk together the grapeseed oil and vanilla extract. Stir the wet ingredients into the almond flour mixture until coarsely blended and crumbly. Sprinkle the topping over the fruit. Cover the dish with aluminum foil.

Bake for 30 minutes. Remove the foil and bake uncovered for an additional 20 minutes, or until the topping is golden brown and the juices are bubbling. Let the crumble cool for 30 minutes, then serve warm.

Coconut Berry Crisp

SERVES 8 ✧ SWEETNESS: MEDIUM

Coconut oil and shredded coconut add a twist to this classic crisp.
My guests are always pleasantly surprised by the complex flavors of
this seemingly simple vegan dessert.

FILLING

2 (10-ounce) packages frozen strawberries

1 (10-ounce) package frozen blueberries

1/4 cup freshly squeezed lemon juice

1 tablespoon agave nectar

2 tablespoons arrowroot powder

TOPPING

1 cup blanched almond flour

1/2 teaspoon sea salt

1/4 teaspoon baking soda

1 cup unsweetened shredded coconut

1 cup walnuts, coarsely chopped

1/2 cup coconut oil, melted over very low heat

1/4 cup agave nectar

Preheat the oven to 350°F. Grease an 8-inch square baking dish with grapeseed oil.

To make the filling, place the frozen berries in the baking dish. Sprinkle with the lemon juice, agave nectar, and arrowroot powder, then gently toss the ingredients to combine.

Bake for 40 to 50 minutes, until the mixture is slightly thickened.

To make the topping, combine the almond flour, salt, baking soda, coconut, and walnuts in a large bowl. In a medium bowl, whisk together the coconut oil and agave nectar. Stir the wet ingredients into the almond flour mixture, until coarsely blended and crumbly. Sprinkle the topping over the fruit.

Bake for 20 to 25 additional minutes, until the topping is golden brown and the juices are bubbling. Let the crisp cool for 30 minutes, then serve warm.

Pear Crisp

SERVES 8 ❖ SWEETNESS: MEDIUM

Looking for a healthy yet tasty dessert? Look no further. With nutrient-dense almond flour and pears, a fruit particularly high in vitamin C, this dish is a great choice. This refreshing crisp is simple, easy to make, and full of warmth and comfort on a chilly fall day. I like to make it with soft, fully ripened pears—Anjou, Bartlett, or Bosc work very well.

FILLING

1/2 cup apple juice

1 tablespoon freshly squeezed lemon juice

1 tablespoon arrowroot powder

1 teaspoon ground nutmeg

5 medium pears, peeled, cored, and sliced 1/4 inch thick

TOPPING

2 cups blanched almond flour

1/2 teaspoon sea salt

1 teaspoon ground cinnamon

1/2 teaspoon ground nutmeg

1/4 cup grapeseed oil

1/4 cup agave nectar

1 tablespoon vanilla extract

❖

Preheat the oven to 350°F. Set aside an 8-inch square baking dish.

To make the filling, whisk together the apple juice, lemon juice, arrowroot powder, and nutmeg in a small bowl. Place the pears in a bowl, toss with the apple juice mixture, then transfer to the baking dish.

To make the topping, combine the almond flour, salt, cinnamon, and nutmeg in a large bowl. In a medium bowl, whisk together the grapeseed oil, agave nectar, and vanilla extract. Stir the wet ingredients into the almond flour mixture, until coarsely blended and crumbly.

Sprinkle the topping over the fruit. Cover the dish with aluminum foil.

Bake for 45 minutes. Remove the foil and bake for an additional 5 to 10 minutes, until the top of the crisp is golden brown and the juices are bubbling. Let the crisp cool for 30 minutes, then serve warm.

Apple Clafoutis

SERVES 8 ❖ SWEETNESS: MEDIUM

My older son and I often make this dish in the fall when local apples
are in season. Have your own little helper prepare the fruit while you
make the batter. Together you can create a delectably elegant dessert
filled with fresh, thinly sliced apples, cinnamon, and a hint of vanilla.
Make this clafoutis with Gala, Fuji, or Braeburn apples, or use Golden
Delicious apples for a sweeter, melt-in-your-mouth clafoutis. For a
dairy-free version, simply replace the heavy cream and butter with
3/4 cup coconut milk.

4 medium apples, peeled, cored, and sliced
1/4 inch thick

4 large eggs

1/4 cup agave nectar

1/2 cup heavy cream

1/4 cup salted butter, melted

1 teaspoon vanilla extract

1/3 cup blanched almond flour

1/4 teaspoon sea salt

1/2 teaspoon ground cinnamon

Preheat the oven to 350°F. Grease a 9-inch
tart pan with grapeseed oil and dust with
almond flour.

Fan the apples in concentric circles on
the bottom of the tart pan.

In a small bowl, whisk together the eggs,
agave nectar, cream, butter, and vanilla
extract. In a medium bowl, combine the
almond flour, salt, and cinnamon. Stir the
wet ingredients into the almond flour mixture until thoroughly combined. Pour the
mixture over the apples.

Bake for 45 to 55 minutes, until the
clafoutis is set in the center and the top is
golden. Let the clafoutis cool for 30 minutes, then serve warm.

Strawberry Crème Tart

SERVES 8 ✥ SWEETNESS: HIGH

Feel free to substitute your favorite fresh fruit at peak season and ripeness for this tart. Plump strawberries in July taste refreshing and look beautiful, though peaches in August work just as well.

¼ cup strawberry fruit spread

1 Simple Tart Crust (page 81), prebaked

1 cup Crème Pâtissière (page 126)

1 quart strawberries, hulled and sliced

Distribute the strawberry fruit spread over the bottom of the cooled crust and place in the refrigerator for 10 minutes to set. Distribute the Crème Pâtissière evenly over the fruit spread. Arrange the strawberry slices in concentric circles over the crème, with the slices slightly overlapping.

Serve immediately, or store in the refrigerator for no longer than 2 hours because the tart will become soggy.

Raspberry Chocolate Chiffon Tart

SERVES 8 ✦ SWEETNESS: HIGH

My husband adores the smooth texture and rich, intense flavor of this elegant chiffon. Top with fresh raspberries, chocolate shavings, and Whipped Cream (page 126) to create a magnificent party-worthy treat.

1 (10-ounce) package frozen raspberries

1/4 cup water

1/2 cup agave nectar

1 tablespoon vanilla extract

1 tablespoon agar flakes

3/4 cup coarsely chopped dark chocolate (73% cacao)

2 egg whites

1 Simple Tart Crust (page 81), prebaked

✦

In a medium saucepan, combine the frozen raspberries and water. Cover and cook over medium heat for 5 minutes, until the raspberries are completely thawed. Remove the mixture from the heat and puree in a blender until smooth. Pour the raspberry mixture through a medium-fine strainer, removing the seeds. Discard the seeds and place the strained raspberries back in the (rinsed) saucepan over medium heat. Add the agave nectar, vanilla extract, and agar flakes, stirring to incorporate. Raise the heat under the saucepan to medium-high and bring the mixture to a rolling boil, stirring frequently for 3 to 5 minutes, until the agar flakes are thoroughly dissolved.

Remove the pan from the heat and place in the refrigerator for 10 to 12 minutes, until slightly cooled but still warm enough to melt the chocolate. Add the chocolate to the raspberry mixture, stirring vigorously until it is completely melted. Place the mixture in the refrigerator for 30 minutes, removing every 5 minutes to scrape down the sides of the pan.

In a large bowl, using a handheld mixer, whip the egg whites to stiff peaks, then gently fold into the cooled raspberry-chocolate mixture. Pour the filling into the cooled tart crust. Place in the refrigerator for 1 hour to set, then serve.

Pie Crust

MAKES ONE 9^1/$_2$-INCH CRUST
SWEETNESS: LOW

All of my crusts are "press-in" pastry, eliminating the extra step of rolling out the dough. They are perfect for tarts, quiches, pies, and tiny appetizers. This basic gluten-free, dairy-free, high-protein crust is one of my staples because it complements a diverse array of pies and treats.

1^1/$_2$ cups blanched almond flour
^{1}/$_4$ teaspoon sea salt
^{1}/$_4$ teaspoon baking soda
^{1}/$_4$ cup grapeseed oil
2 tablespoons agave nectar
1 teaspoon vanilla extract

Preheat the oven to 350°F.

    In a large bowl, combine the almond flour, salt, and baking soda. In a medium bowl, whisk together the grapeseed oil, agave nectar, and vanilla extract. Stir the wet ingredients into the almond flour mixture until thoroughly combined. Press the dough into a 9^1/$_2$-inch or deep-dish pie pan.

    Bake for 10 to 15 minutes, until golden brown. Remove from the oven and let cool completely before filling.

Dark Chocolate Pie Crust

MAKES ONE 9^1/$_2$-INCH CRUST
SWEETNESS: MEDIUM

This deep dark chocolate crust makes an alluring base for your favorite pies. Pair with Pecan Pie (page 68) or one of your own creations.

1^1/$_4$ cups blanched almond flour
^{1}/$_4$ teaspoon sea salt
^{1}/$_4$ teaspoon baking soda
2 tablespoons grapeseed oil
2 tablespoons agave nectar
^{1}/$_2$ cup chopped dark chocolate (73% cacao), melted over very low heat

Preheat the oven to 350°F.

    In a large bowl, combine the almond flour, salt, and baking soda. In a medium bowl, whisk together the grapeseed oil, agave nectar, and melted chocolate. Stir the wet ingredients into the almond flour mixture until thoroughly combined. Press the dough into a 9^1/$_2$-inch or deep-dish pie pan.

    Bake for 8 to 12 minutes, until the surface of the crust loses its sheen and starts to look dry—be careful not to overcook. Remove from the oven and let cool completely before filling.

Coconut Pie Crust

MAKES ONE 9¹/₂-INCH CRUST ✦

SWEETNESS: LOW

This crust is divine with Chocolate Cream Pie (page 71), or create your own Key lime filling for a fruity treat.

1½ ³/₄ cup blanched almond flour

½ ¹/₄ teaspoon sea salt

1½ ³/₄ cup unsweetened shredded coconut, toasted

½ ¹/₄ cup coconut oil, melted over very low heat

2 1 tablespoon agave nectar   *Xylitol Syrup*

2 1 teaspoon vanilla extract

Preheat the oven to 350°F.

In a large bowl, combine the almond flour, salt, and shredded coconut. In a medium bowl, whisk together the coconut oil, agave nectar, and vanilla extract. Stir the wet ingredients into the almond flour mixture until thoroughly combined. Press the dough into a 9¹/₂-inch or deep-dish pie pan.

Bake for 7 to 12 minutes, until golden brown. Remove from the oven and let cool completely before filling.

Crunchy Almond Pie Crust

MAKES ONE 9¹/₂-INCH CRUST ✦

SWEETNESS: LOW

Be sure to use almond slivers in this recipe, not almond slices. The almond slivers add texture to the crust, making your standard pies crunchy and unique. My favorite way to serve this crust is as the base for Chocolate Cream Pie (page 71).

1 cup blanched almond flour

1/2 cup coarsely chopped almond slivers

1/4 teaspoon sea salt

1/4 cup grapeseed oil

2 tablespoons agave nectar

1 teaspoon vanilla extract

Preheat the oven to 350°F.

In a large bowl, combine the almond flour, almonds, and salt. In a medium bowl, whisk together the grapeseed oil, agave nectar, and vanilla extract. Stir the wet ingredients into the almond flour mixture until thoroughly combined. Press the dough into a 9¹/₂-inch or deep-dish pie pan.

Bake for 12 to 15 minutes, until golden brown. Remove from the oven and let cool completely before filling.

◀

Simple Tart Crust

MAKES ONE 9-INCH CRUST ❖
SWEETNESS: LOW

Who knew that a simple tart crust could be health food in disguise? Using heart-healthy almond flour in your crusts lowers the glycemic index of your favorite desserts. High-protein almond flour also steadies the absorption of carbohydrates from a sweet filling.

$1^1/_2$ cups blanched almond flour
$^1/_2$ teaspoon sea salt
$^1/_4$ teaspoon baking soda
$^1/_4$ cup grapeseed oil
2 tablespoons agave nectar

Preheat the oven to 350°F.

In a large bowl, combine the almond flour, salt, and baking soda. In a medium bowl, whisk together the grapeseed oil and agave nectar. Stir the wet ingredients into the almond flour mixture until thoroughly combined. Press the dough into a 9-inch tart pan.

Bake for 7 to 10 minutes, until golden brown. Remove from the oven and let cool completely before filling.

Savory Pie Crust

MAKES ONE $9^1/_2$-INCH CRUST

This gluten-free, dairy-free almond flour crust adds extra nutrition to your favorite quiche recipe. When I make Chicken Pot Pie (page 43), I often use parsley in place of the scallions for this crust.

$1^1/_2$ cups blanched almond flour
$^1/_2$ teaspoon sea salt
$^1/_2$ teaspoon baking soda
1 tablespoon minced scallions (white and green parts)
$^1/_4$ cup grapeseed oil
1 tablespoon water

Preheat the oven to 350°F.

In a large bowl, combine the almond flour, salt, baking soda, and scallions. In a medium bowl, whisk together the grapeseed oil and water. Stir the wet ingredients into the almond flour mixture until thoroughly combined. Press the dough into a $9^1/_2$-inch or deep-dish pie pan.

Bake for 12 to 15 minutes, until golden brown. Remove from the oven and let cool completely before filling.

Herb Tart Crust

MAKES ONE 9-INCH CRUST

The rosemary version of this Herb Tart Crust pairs perfectly with either my Spinach Sun-Dried Tomato Tart (page 64) or Kale Tart with Cranberries (page 63). Use the scallion version for the Smoked Salmon–Leek Tart (page 52), or whip up a tart creation of your own by filling this crust with your favorite sautéed veggies.

1¹/₂ cups blanched almond flour

¹/₂ teaspoon sea salt

1 tablespoon minced fresh rosemary or scallions (white and green parts)

¹/₄ cup grapeseed oil

1 tablespoon water

Preheat the oven to 350°F.

In a large bowl, combine the almond flour, salt, and rosemary or scallions. In a medium bowl, whisk together the grapeseed oil and water. Stir the wet ingredients into the almond flour mixture until thoroughly combined. Press the dough into a 9-inch tart pan.

Bake for 15 to 20 minutes, until golden brown. Remove from the oven and let cool completely before filling.

Pizza Crust

MAKES ONE 10-INCH CRUST

If you are timid about cooking, pizza is a good place to start. Pair this crust with your favorite toppings to create any number of pizza variations. Or, if you're looking for a sure bet, use it with my Broccoli Pizza (page 57).

1¹/₂ cups blanched almond flour _[handwritten: 3/4]_

¹/₄ teaspoon sea salt _[handwritten: 1/8]_

¹/₄ teaspoon baking soda _[handwritten: 1/8]_

1 tablespoon grapeseed oil _[handwritten: 1¹/₂ tsp]_

1 large egg _[handwritten: small egg]_

Preheat the oven to 350°F. Set aside a large baking sheet. Cut 2 pieces of parchment paper to the size of the baking sheet.

In a large bowl, combine the almond flour, salt, and baking soda. In a medium bowl, whisk together the grapeseed oil and egg. Stir the wet ingredients into the almond flour mixture until thoroughly combined.

Place the dough between the 2 sheets of parchment paper and roll into a 10-inch circle, ¹/₈ inch thick. Remove the top piece of parchment paper and transfer the bottom piece of parchment paper with the rolled-out dough onto the baking sheet.

Bake for 15 to 20 minutes, until lightly golden. Remove from the oven and add toppings while still warm.

Cakes and Cupcakes

Chocolate Cake

SERVES 8 ✤ SWEETNESS: HIGH

Chocolate Cake with fluffy Marshmallow Frosting (page 125) is a fabulous birthday treat for children and adults alike. To make a layer cake, simply double the recipe below and use two cake pans.

2 cups blanched almond flour

1/4 cup unsweetened cocoa powder

1/2 teaspoon sea salt

1/2 teaspoon baking soda

1 cup agave nectar

2 large eggs

1 tablespoon vanilla extract

Preheat the oven to 350°F. Grease a 9-inch cake pan with grapeseed oil and dust with almond flour.

In a large bowl, combine the almond flour, cocoa powder, salt, and baking soda. In a medium bowl, combine the agave nectar, eggs, and vanilla extract. Stir the wet ingredients into the almond flour mixture until thoroughly combined. Scoop the batter into the prepared cake pan.

Bake for 35 to 40 minutes, until a toothpick inserted into the center of the cake comes out clean. Let the cake cool in the pan for 1 hour, then serve.

Chocolate Chip Banana Cake

SERVES 8 ✦ SWEETNESS: HIGH

Chocolate chunks transform this cake from standard fare into a decadent dessert. If you're looking for a light and simple banana cake, feel free to make this recipe sans chocolate.

3 cups blanched almond flour

1/2 teaspoon sea salt

1 teaspoon baking soda

1/4 cup grapeseed oil

1/4 cup agave nectar

3 large eggs

1 tablespoon vanilla extract

1 cup coarsely chopped dark chocolate (73% cacao)

1 cup (2 to 3) mashed very ripe bananas

Preheat the oven to 350°F. Grease a 9-inch cake pan with grapeseed oil and dust with almond flour.

In a large bowl, combine the almond flour, salt, and baking soda. In a medium bowl, whisk together the grapeseed oil, agave nectar, eggs, and vanilla extract. Stir the wet ingredients into the almond flour mixture until thoroughly combined. Fold in the chocolate and bananas. Scoop the batter into the prepared cake pan.

Bake for 35 to 45 minutes, until a toothpick inserted into the center of the cake comes out clean. Let the cake cool in the pan for 1 hour, then serve.

Spice Cake

SERVES 12 ✤ SWEETNESS: HIGH

When I think of dessert, spice cake is not necessarily the first thing that comes to mind. However, my friend Patricia told me this cookbook would not be complete without it. Luckily, Patricia gave my Spice Cake her stamp of approval and suggested topping it with crème fraîche or Whipped Cream (page 126).

2 1/2 cups blanched almond flour

1/2 teaspoon sea salt

1/2 teaspoon baking soda

1 tablespoon ground cinnamon

1 teaspoon ground allspice

1 teaspoon ground nutmeg

1/4 teaspoon ground cloves

1/4 cup grapeseed oil

1 cup agave nectar

3 large eggs

1 tablespoon vanilla extract

1 cup prunes, chopped into 1/4-inch pieces

1/2 cup walnuts, coarsely chopped

Preheat the oven to 350°F. Grease an 8-inch square baking dish with grapeseed oil and dust with almond flour.

In a large bowl, combine the almond flour, salt, baking soda, cinnamon, allspice, nutmeg, and cloves. In a medium bowl, whisk together the grapeseed oil, agave nectar, eggs, and vanilla extract. Stir the wet ingredients into the almond flour mixture until thoroughly combined. Fold in the prunes and walnuts. Scoop the batter into the prepared baking dish.

Bake for 40 to 45 minutes, until a toothpick inserted into the center of the cake comes out clean. Let the cake cool in the baking dish for 1 hour, then serve.

Classic Carrot Cake

SERVES 12 ❖ SWEETNESS: MEDIUM

This rich, moist carrot cake is a healthy high-protein dessert. Serve plain or with Creamy Coconut Frosting (page 125) spread over the top and sides of the cake. For an extra-special treat, sprinkle with toasted shredded coconut.

3 cups blanched almond flour
2 teaspoons sea salt
1 teaspoon baking soda
1 tablespoon ground cinnamon
1 teaspoon ground nutmeg
1/4 cup grapeseed oil
1/2 cup agave nectar
5 large eggs
3 cups grated carrots
1 cup raisins
1 cup walnuts, coarsely chopped

Preheat the oven to 325°F. Grease two 9-inch cake pans with grapeseed oil and dust with almond flour.

In a large bowl, combine the almond flour, salt, baking soda, cinnamon, and nutmeg. In a medium bowl, whisk together the grapeseed oil, agave nectar, and eggs. Stir the wet ingredients into the almond flour mixture until thoroughly combined. Fold in the carrots, raisins, and walnuts. Scoop the batter into the prepared cake pans.

Bake for 30 to 35 minutes, until a toothpick inserted into the center of the cake comes out clean. Let the cakes cool in the pans for 1 hour, then serve.

Chocolate Velvet Torte

SERVES 12 ✤ SWEETNESS: HIGH

Light yet rich, this decadent torte recipe is based on one in *Joy of Cooking* called "Queen of Sheba." Although this is one of my more complex recipes, the results are well worth the process. Be sure to use the best-quality organic chocolate you can find for this recipe— it makes all the difference.

1 cup coarsely chopped dark chocolate (73% cacao)

1/2 cup grapeseed oil

6 large eggs, separated

1/2 cup agave nectar

1/2 teaspoon almond extract

1/4 teaspoon cream of tartar

1/2 cup blanched almond flour, sifted

1/2 teaspoon sea salt

✤

Preheat the oven to 350°F. Grease a 9-inch springform pan with grapeseed oil and dust with almond flour.

In a small pan over the lowest heat possible, melt the chocolate until smooth. Stir in the grapeseed oil and remove from the heat. Set the mixture aside.

In a large bowl, whisk together the egg yolks, agave nectar, and almond extract until thick and pale yellow. Whisk the chocolate mixture into the egg yolk mixture. In a separate bowl, whip the egg whites and cream of tartar to stiff peaks with a handheld mixer.

In another bowl, combine the almond flour and salt. Gently fold the almond flour mixture into the chocolate mixture, and then fold in the egg white mixture. Scoop the batter into the prepared springform pan and spread evenly.

Bake until a toothpick inserted 1 inch from the edge of the cake comes out clean, 25 to 30 minutes; the center will remain moist and quite gooey. Allow the cake to cool completely, about 1 hour; the center will sink, this is normal. Slide a thin knife around the torte to detach it from the pan. Invert the torte onto a plate and serve.

Vanilla Raspberry Torte

SERVES 12 ✧ SWEETNESS: HIGH

Moist, dense vanilla cake layers alternate with a delightfully tangy raspberry filling; the finishing touch is a rich chocolate frosting that completely envelops this elegant dessert. For the raspberry fruit spread, use a high-quality, 100% organic, juice-sweetened product. You can purchase coconut flour online, and it's also readily available in most health food stores.

2 cups blanched almond flour
1/4 cup coconut flour
1/2 teaspoon sea salt
1 3/4 cups agave nectar
10 large eggs
1 tablespoon vanilla extract
1/2 cup raspberry fruit spread
1 1/2 cups Chocolate Frosting (page 124)

✧

Preheat the oven to 350°F. Line the bottoms of 3 (9-inch) cake pans with parchment paper.

In a medium bowl, combine the almond flour, coconut flour, and salt. In a large bowl, whisk together the agave nectar, eggs, and vanilla extract. Gently fold the almond flour mixture into the wet ingredients and blend well (the batter will be thin). Divide the cake batter evenly among the 3 prepared cake pans, about 2 cups per pan.

Bake for 20 to 25 minutes, until the cakes are golden brown and a toothpick inserted into the center of each cake comes out clean. Let the cakes cool in the pans for at least 1 hour. Run a knife around the edge of the cakes to loosen them from the pans. Remove from the pans and peel off the parchment.

Place the bottom layer of the cake on a serving plate and cover with 1/4 cup of the raspberry spread. Add the next layer of cake and cover with the remaining raspberry spread. Add the third layer of cake. Frost the top and sides with Chocolate Frosting before serving.

Strawberry Shortcake

SERVES 8 ✦ SWEETNESS: MEDIUM

When I concocted this Strawberry Shortcake bright and early one morning, I ate it for breakfast. I just couldn't help myself, in spite of the fact that I am a big fan of starting off the day with protein. This is one of my favorite dishes. It works well with any fresh, seasonal fruit— try blueberries in June or peaches in August.

8 Classic Drop Biscuits (page 20), prebaked
4 cups Whipped Cream (page 126)
1 pint fresh strawberries, hulled and sliced

Cut each biscuit in half horizontally. Place the bottom halves of the biscuits on individual serving plates. Place a heaping tablespoon of the whipped cream and then several strawberry slices onto each biscuit half. Add another layer of the cream, then top with the remaining biscuit halves. Spoon a generous dollop of Whipped Cream and strawberries onto the top of each biscuit and serve right after assembling.

Icebox Cake

SERVES 8 ✦ SWEETNESS: HIGH

This dessert dates back to the 1930s when Nabisco suggested layering their chocolate wafers with whipped cream to make an "elegant" dessert. The instructions were simple and brief: Stack the wafers to form a log with whipped cream cementing them together and then lay the log on its side. I've given you a few extra steps to provide further detail. When you cut this cake, start at one end and slice on the diagonal to get a zebralike stripe in each piece. My friends Chris and Larry love this Icebox Cake—they say it tastes like Ho Hos.

2 cups heavy cream
1/4 cup agave nectar
1 tablespoon vanilla extract
12 Chewy Chocolate Cookies (page 102)
1/4 cup grated dark chocolate (73% cacao)

✦

In a large bowl, whip together the cream, agave nectar, and vanilla extract until the cream begins to thicken and soft peaks form. Spread a scant 1/4 cup of the whipped cream mixture between 2 cookies, making 6 sandwiches in all. Spoon a thin layer of whipped cream onto a pretty serving platter. Cement the cookie sandwiches together with more whipped cream and stand them back to back on their edges like a row of dominoes to form a log on the platter.

When all 12 cookies are lined up, spread the remaining whipped cream over the entire log. Place the cake in the refrigerator for 5 hours or overnight (no need to cover it, you don't want to dent or smudge the fluffy whipped frosting).

Remove from the refrigerator and dust with grated chocolate. Cut the cake on the diagonal at a 45-degree angle so that stripes of chocolate and cream appear in each slice, then serve.

Very Vanilla Cupcakes

MAKES 10 CUPCAKES ❖ SWEETNESS: MEDIUM

Whenever I have these on the counter, Josh, one of the children in our neighborhood, grabs a handful as he passes through the kitchen in search of my boys. "Sit down while you eat!" I call after him as he runs out the back door. Loot in hand, he doesn't even wait for me to top them with Chocolate Frosting (page 124).

2 large eggs, separated
1/4 cup grapeseed oil
1/2 cup agave nectar
1 tablespoon vanilla extract
1 tablespoon freshly squeezed lemon juice
2 1/2 cups blanched almond flour
1/2 teaspoon sea salt
1/2 teaspoon baking soda

Preheat the oven to 350°F. Line 10 muffin cups with paper liners.

In a large bowl, whisk the egg yolks until pale yellow with a handheld mixer, then whisk in the grapeseed oil, agave nectar, vanilla extract, and lemon juice. In a medium bowl, whisk the egg whites to stiff peaks with a handheld mixer. Gently fold the egg whites into the yolk mixture.

In a separate bowl, combine the almond flour, salt, and baking soda, then gently fold into the egg mixture. Scoop the batter into the prepared muffin cups.

Bake for 20 to 30 minutes, until the tops are golden brown or a toothpick inserted into the center of a cupcake comes out clean. Let the cupcakes cool in the pan for 30 minutes; the center will sink just a bit—this is normal. Frost, if desired, then serve.

Vanilla Cupcakes with Raspberry Fig Filling

MAKES 24 MINI-CUPCAKES ✦ SWEETNESS: HIGH

Inside each of these mini-cupcakes is a pocketful of tart yet sweet raspberry-fig filling. Everyone who tries these fails to stop at just one! I make a habit of using organic, purely fruit-sweetened spread for this recipe. Such healthy, delicious spreads are a staple in my pantry.

CUPCAKE BATTER

3 cups blanched almond flour

1/2 teaspoon sea salt

1/2 teaspoon baking soda

1/4 cup grapeseed oil

1/2 cup agave nectar

2 large eggs

1 tablespoon vanilla extract

1/2 teaspoon apple cider vinegar

1/4 teaspoon orange zest

FILLING

1/2 cup dried figs

1/2 cup raspberry fruit spread

✦

Preheat the oven to 350°F. Line 24 mini-muffin cups with paper liners.

To make the batter, combine the almond flour, salt, and baking soda in a large bowl.

In a medium bowl, whisk together the grapeseed oil, agave nectar, eggs, vanilla extract, vinegar, and orange zest. Stir the wet ingredients into the almond flour mixture until thoroughly combined.

To make the filling, place the figs in a food processor and pulse to a fine paste. Gradually pulse in the raspberry fruit spread.

Scoop 1 heaping teaspoon of batter into each lined mini-muffin cup. Drop 1 teaspoon of the raspberry-fig mixture into the batter. Cover the filling by scooping an additional heaping teaspoon of batter onto each cupcake.

Bake for 12 to 17 minutes, until a toothpick inserted into the center of a cupcake comes out clean. Let the cupcakes cool in the pan for 30 minutes, then serve.

Cookies and Bars

Elana's Chocolate Chip Cookies

MAKES 30 COOKIES ❖ SWEETNESS: MEDIUM

These moist, chewy cookies travel well and are my go-to treat for potlucks and picnics. A scoop of vanilla ice cream between two of these cookies makes a fabulously rich ice cream sandwich.

2½ cups blanched almond flour

½ teaspoon sea salt

½ teaspoon baking soda

½ cup grapeseed oil

½ cup agave nectar

1 tablespoon vanilla extract

½ cup coarsely chopped dark chocolate (73% cacao)

Preheat the oven to 350°F. Line 2 large baking sheets with parchment paper.

In a large bowl, combine the almond flour, salt, and baking soda. In a medium bowl, whisk together the grapeseed oil, agave nectar, and vanilla extract. Stir the wet ingredients into the almond flour mixture until thoroughly combined. Fold in the chocolate, then refrigerate the dough for 20 minutes. Spoon the dough 1 heaping tablespoon at a time onto the prepared baking sheets, pressing down with the palm of your hand to flatten, leaving 2 inches between each cookie.

Bake for 7 to 10 minutes, until lightly golden. Let the cookies cool on the baking sheets for 20 minutes, then serve warm.

Tropical Chocolate Chip Cookies

MAKES 36 COOKIES   ◆   SWEETNESS: MEDIUM

This fun twist on classic chocolate chip cookies adds tropical flavor and crunch to everyone's favorite treat.

3T coconut flour or more

2 1/2 cups blanched almond flour

1/2 teaspoon sea salt

1/2 teaspoon baking soda

1/2 cup coconut oil, melted over very low heat

(1/2 cup agave nectar) *2 eggs*

1 tablespoon vanilla extract

1/2 cup coarsely chopped dark chocolate (73% cacao)

1/2 cup cashews, toasted and coarsely chopped *pecans*

1/2 cup unsweetened shredded coconut, toasted

1/4 c Erythritol
1/2 tsp stevia

Preheat the oven to 350°F. Line 2 large baking sheets with parchment paper.

In a large bowl, combine the almond flour, salt, and baking soda. In a medium bowl, combine the coconut oil, agave nectar, and vanilla extract. Stir the wet ingredients into the almond flour mixture until thoroughly combined. Fold in the chocolate, cashews, and coconut. Spoon the dough 1 heaping tablespoon at a time onto the prepared baking sheets, pressing down with the palm of your hand to flatten, leaving 2 inches between each cookie.

Bake for 7 to 10 minutes, until lightly golden. Let the cookies cool on the baking sheets for 20 minutes, then serve warm.

Double Chocolate Cherry Cookies

MAKES 24 COOKIES ❖ SWEETNESS: HIGH

These chocolaty cookies are a favorite in my household and vanish from my countertop in no time flat. The double dose of dark antioxidant-rich chocolate along with almond flour (rich in cholesterol-lowering omega fatty acids) makes these cookies a heart-healthy treat.

2 3/4 cups blanched almond flour

1/2 teaspoon sea salt

1/2 teaspoon baking soda

1/4 cup unsweetened cocoa powder

1/2 cup grapeseed oil

3/4 cup agave nectar

1 tablespoon vanilla extract

1 cup coarsely chopped dark chocolate (73% cacao)

1 cup dried fruit-juice-sweetened cherries

Preheat the oven to 350°F. Line 2 large baking sheets with parchment paper.

In a large bowl, combine the almond flour, salt, baking soda, and cocoa powder. In a medium bowl, whisk together the grapeseed oil, agave nectar, and vanilla extract. Fold the wet ingredients into the almond flour mixture until thoroughly combined. Fold in the chocolate and cherries. Spoon the dough 1 heaping tablespoon at a time onto the prepared baking sheets, leaving 2 inches between each cookie.

Bake for 10 to 15 minutes, until the tops of the cookies look dry and start to crack—be careful not to overcook. Let the cookies cool on the baking sheets for 20 minutes, then serve warm.

Chewy Chocolate Cookies

MAKES 12 COOKIES ❖ SWEETNESS: MEDIUM

Use these versatile chocolate cookies for Icebox Cake (page 93). Or, to create the perfect sandwich cookie: reduce their size by spooning the dough 1 tablespoon at a time onto a baking sheet, bake for 8 to 10 minutes, cool, then spread frosting between two cookies. For whoopie pies, smother Marshmallow Frosting (page 125) between two cookies. Whatever you make, be sure to frost just before eating in order to maintain the consistency of these cookies.

3 cups blanched almond flour

1/2 teaspoon sea salt

1 teaspoon baking soda

1/2 cup arrowroot powder

1/4 cup unsweetened cocoa powder

1/2 cup grapeseed oil

3/4 cup agave nectar

1 tablespoon vanilla extract

Preheat the oven to 350°F. Line 2 large baking sheets with parchment paper.

In a large bowl, combine the almond flour, salt, baking soda, arrowroot powder, and cocoa powder. In a medium bowl, whisk together the grapeseed oil, agave nectar, and vanilla extract. Stir the wet ingredients into the almond flour mixture until thoroughly combined. Scoop the dough a scant 1/4 cup at a time onto the prepared baking sheets, leaving 2 inches between each cookie.

Bake for 10 to 15 minutes, until the tops of the cookies look dry and start to crack—be careful not to overcook. Let the cookies cool on the baking sheets for 30 minutes and spread with frosting just before serving.

Snickerdoodles

MAKES 36 COOKIES ◈ SWEETNESS: MEDIUM

Since Snickerdoodles are such a classic cookie, I was pleased to finally add this vegan version to my repertoire. Let these cool on the counter overnight and then store in an airtight container to maintain freshness— they will keep for three to four days.

2$1/2$ cups blanched almond flour

$1/2$ teaspoon sea salt

1 teaspoon baking soda

$1/2$ cup arrowroot powder

6 tablespoons grapeseed oil

$1/2$ cup agave nectar

2 tablespoons vanilla extract

Ground cinnamon, for topping

Preheat the oven to 350°F. Line 2 large baking sheets with parchment paper.

In a large bowl, combine the almond flour, salt, baking soda, and arrowroot powder. In a medium bowl, whisk together the grapeseed oil, agave nectar, and vanilla extract. Stir the wet ingredients into the almond flour mixture until thoroughly combined. Spoon the dough 1 tablespoon at a time onto the prepared baking sheets, pressing down with the palm of your hand to flatten, leaving 2 inches between each cookie. Sprinkle the cookies with cinnamon.

Bake for 7 to 10 minutes, until lightly golden. Let the cookies cool on the baking sheets for 30 minutes, then serve.

Rosemary Hazelnut Shortbread Cookies

MAKES 24 COOKIES ✦ SWEETNESS: MEDIUM

These cookies are a little off the wall for me, since I usually stick to more traditional, classic flavors. However, one very popular French blogger made rosemary hazelnut tuiles (light and delicate whispers of a cookie) a couple of years back on National Public Radio, inspiring me to try the combination of rosemary and hazelnut in a more substantial cookie.

2^1/$_2$ cups blanched almond flour

^{1}/$_2$ teaspoon sea salt

^{1}/$_2$ teaspoon baking soda

1 cup hazelnuts, toasted and coarsely chopped

1 tablespoon finely chopped fresh rosemary

^{1}/$_2$ cup grapeseed oil

5 tablespoons agave nectar

1 tablespoon vanilla extract

✦

Preheat the oven to 350°F. Line 2 large baking sheets with parchment paper.

In a large bowl, combine the almond flour, salt, baking soda, hazelnuts, and rosemary. In a medium bowl, whisk together the grapeseed oil, agave nectar, and vanilla extract. Stir the wet ingredients into the almond flour mixture until thoroughly combined.

Roll the dough into a large log, 2^1/$_2$ inches in diameter, then wrap in parchment paper. Place in the freezer for 1 hour, or until firm. Remove the log from the freezer, unwrap it, and cut it into ^{1}/$_4$-inch-thick slices with a wet knife. Transfer the slices onto the prepared baking sheets, leaving 2 inches between each cookie.

Bake for 7 to 10 minutes, until brown around the edges. Let the cookies cool on the baking sheets for 30 minutes, then serve.

Pecan Shortbread Cookies

MAKES 24 COOKIES ◆ SWEETNESS: MEDIUM

This has been one of my favorite cookies since childhood; back then they were known as Pecan Sandies. This dairy-free, lightly-sweetened version is every bit as good.

2^1/$_2$ cups blanched almond flour

^{1}/$_2$ teaspoon sea salt

^{1}/$_4$ teaspoon baking soda

1 cup pecans, toasted and coarsely chopped

^{1}/$_2$ cup grapeseed oil

5 tablespoons agave nectar

1 tablespoon vanilla extract

Preheat the oven to 350°F. Line 2 large baking sheets with parchment paper.

In a large bowl, combine the almond flour, salt, baking soda, and pecans. In a medium bowl, whisk together the grapeseed oil, agave nectar, and vanilla extract. Stir the wet ingredients into the almond flour mixture until thoroughly combined.

Roll the dough into a large log, 2^1/$_2$ inches in diameter, then wrap it in parchment paper. Place in the freezer for 1 hour, or until firm. Remove the log from the freezer, unwrap it, and cut it into ^{1}/$_8$-inch-thick slices with a wet knife. Transfer the slices onto the prepared baking sheets, leaving 2 inches between each cookie.

Bake for 7 to 10 minutes, until lightly golden. Let the cookies cool on the baking sheets for 1 hour, then serve.

Holiday Cookies

MAKES 24 COOKIES ✦ SWEETNESS: MEDIUM

Use stars, trees, hearts, and other cookie-cutter shapes to make these the perfect treat for any holiday. Spread with Creamy Coconut Frosting (page 125) and decorate with dried fruit or sprinkles.

2 1/2 cups blanched almond flour
1/2 teaspoon sea salt
1/2 cup grapeseed oil
1/4 cup agave nectar
1 tablespoon vanilla extract

Preheat the oven to 350°F. Line 2 large baking sheets with parchment paper.

In a large bowl, combine the almond flour and salt. In a medium bowl, whisk together the grapeseed oil, agave nectar, and vanilla extract. Stir the wet ingredients into the almond flour mixture until thoroughly combined.

Place the dough in the freezer for 1 hour. Roll out the dough to 1/2-inch thickness between 2 sheets of parchment paper. If the dough is sticky, dust it with almond flour. Remove the top piece of parchment paper and cut out the cookies with a holiday cookie cutter, dipping it in cold water after cutting each cookie to prevent sticking. Transfer the cookies onto the prepared baking sheets, leaving 2 inches between each cookie.

Bake for 7 to 10 minutes, until lightly golden. Let the cookies cool on the baking sheets for 1 hour, then serve.

Gingerbread Men

MAKES 24 COOKIES ❖ SWEETNESS: MEDIUM

Children love making these holiday treats. My boys decorate them with dried currants, raisins, and dried cranberries, and use slivered almonds to make little mouths. On a nutritional note, I often use yacon syrup in place of molasses in my recipes. Yacon root is high in fiber and rich in prebiotics, which aid in the beginning stages of digestion.

3 cups blanched almond flour

1 tablespoon ground cinnamon

1¼ teaspoons ground ginger

¼ teaspoon sea salt

½ teaspoon baking soda

¼ teaspoon ground cloves

¼ cup grapeseed oil

¼ cup agave nectar

1 tablespoon vanilla extract

¼ cup yacon syrup

1 large egg

1 teaspoon lemon zest

❖

Preheat the oven to 350°F. Line 2 large baking sheets with parchment paper.

In a large bowl, combine the almond flour, cinnamon, ginger, salt, baking soda, and cloves. In a medium bowl, whisk together the grapeseed oil, agave nectar, vanilla extract, yacon syrup, egg, and lemon zest. Stir the wet ingredients into the almond flour mixture until thoroughly combined. Cover the dough and let chill in the freezer overnight.

Roll out the dough to ½-inch thickness between 2 sheets of parchment paper. If the dough is sticky, dust it with almond flour. Remove the top sheet of parchment paper and cut out the cookies using a gingerbread man cookie cutter (to prevent sticking, dip it in cold water after cutting each cookie). Transfer the cookies onto the prepared baking sheets, leaving 2 inches between each cookie.

Bake for 8 to 12 minutes, until lightly browned around the edges. Let the cookies cool on the baking sheets for 30 minutes, then serve warm.

Hamantaschen

Hamantaschen are traditionally served during the Jewish festival of Purim. Growing up I was taught that hamantaschen symbolize Haman's hat—the triangular type worn during the first Persian Empire.

FILLING

1 cup dried currants

1^1/$_2$ cups water

2 medium apples, peeled, cored, and diced into ^{1}/$_4$-inch cubes

1 whole vanilla bean

6 slivers lemon rind, 1-inch long by ^{1}/$_4$-inch wide

1 cup dried apricots, chopped into ^{1}/$_4$-inch pieces

DOUGH

3 cups blanched almond flour

^{1}/$_2$ teaspoon sea salt

^{1}/$_2$ cup grapeseed oil

2 tablespoons agave nectar

1 large egg

1 tablespoon vanilla extract

✧

Preheat the oven to 350°F. Line 3 large baking sheets with parchment paper.

To make the filling, puree the currants and water in a blender until smooth. In a medium saucepan, combine the currant mixture, apples, vanilla bean, lemon rind, and dried apricots. Cook over medium heat, stirring occasionally, until the apples are soft, about 45 minutes. Remove the vanilla bean.

To make the dough, combine the almond flour and salt in a large bowl. In a medium bowl, whisk together the grapeseed oil, agave nectar, egg, and vanilla extract. Stir the wet ingredients into the almond flour mixture until thoroughly combined.

Roll the dough into 1-inch balls and press onto the prepared baking sheets to form ^{1}/$_8$-inch-thick disks, leaving 2 inches between each. Scoop 1 teaspoon of the filling onto each circle of dough. Fold the dough in from 3 sides and pinch the corners to form a triangle.

Bake for 10 to 15 minutes, until lightly golden. Let the cookies cool on the baking sheets for 1 hour, then serve.

Fig Newtons

MAKES 20 COOKIES ✦ SWEETNESS: HIGH

Fig Newtons remind me of childhood. With almond flour, I can enjoy them once again—without the spike in blood sugar.

FILLING

1 cup dried figs

$1/4$ cup freshly squeezed lemon juice

1 tablespoon vanilla extract

DOUGH

$2^1/2$ cups blanched almond flour

$1/2$ teaspoon sea salt

$1/4$ cup grapeseed oil

$1/2$ cup agave nectar

$1/4$ cup yacon syrup

1 tablespoon vanilla extract

✦

Preheat the oven to 350°F. Line 2 large baking sheets with parchment paper.

To make the filling, blend the figs in a food processor until well chopped, about 30 seconds. Add the lemon juice and vanilla extract. Process until a smooth paste forms. Set the filling aside until ready to use.

To make the dough, combine the almond flour and salt in a large bowl. In a medium bowl, whisk together the grape-seed oil, agave nectar, yacon syrup, and vanilla extract. Stir the wet ingredients into the almond flour mixture until thoroughly combined. Refrigerate the dough for 1 hour.

Divide the chilled dough into 4 parts. Place 1 piece of dough between 2 sheets of parchment paper and roll the dough into a 10 by 4-inch rectangle, $1/4$ inch thick. If the dough is wet, dust it with almond flour. Spread one-fourth of the filling evenly down the long side of the rectangle. Fold the dough in half lengthwise, resulting in a 10 by 2-inch bar. Mend the seam where the two sides of dough come together so that the bar is symmetrical. Repeat this process with the 3 remaining parts of the dough and the filling.

Transfer 2 bars to each prepared baking sheet. Bake for 15 to 18 minutes, until lightly golden. Let the bars cool on the baking sheets for 30 minutes before cutting into 2-inch squares.

Almond Macaroons

MAKES 20 COOKIES ✧ SWEETNESS: MEDIUM

This standard French treat has become quite popular and is often written up in fancy food magazines. You will see why when you taste these sweet bonbon-like little cookies that are full of intense marzipan flavor.

1 egg white
¼ cup agave nectar
1 teaspoon lemon zest
1 tablespoon almond extract
2 cups blanched almond flour
⅛ teaspoon sea salt

Preheat the oven to 350°F. Line a large baking sheet with parchment paper.

In a large bowl, whisk the egg white to stiff peaks with a handheld mixer. Whisk in the agave nectar, lemon zest, and almond extract. Fold the almond flour and salt into the wet mixture. Spoon the dough 1 tablespoon at a time onto the prepared baking sheet, leaving 2 inches between each macaroon.

Bake for 10 to 12 minutes, until lightly golden. Let the cookies cool on the baking sheet for 1 hour, then serve.

Chocolate Coconut Macaroons

MAKES 24 COOKIES ✦ SWEETNESS: HIGH

I grew up eating overly sweet Manischewitz macaroons from the can each year at our Passover Seders. These classic coconut macaroons with a chocolate twist definitely trump those of my childhood.

1¹/2 cups blanched almond flour

¹/2 teaspoon sea salt

2 cups unsweetened shredded coconut

¹/4 cup unsweetened cocoa powder

3 egg whites

1 cup agave nectar

Preheat the oven to 350°F. Line 2 large baking sheets with parchment paper.

In a large bowl, combine the almond flour, salt, coconut, and cocoa powder. In a medium bowl, whisk the egg whites to stiff peaks with a handheld mixer. Blend in the agave nectar. Fold the wet ingredients into the almond flour mixture. Spoon the dough 1 tablespoon at a time onto the prepared baking sheets, leaving 2 inches between each macaroon.

Bake for 15 to 20 minutes, until golden around the edges. Let the cookies cool on the baking sheets for 30 minutes, then serve.

Chocolate Cranberry Biscotti

MAKES 24 BISCOTTI ✧ SWEETNESS: MEDIUM

Biscotti are elegant yet simple biscuits that satisfy every adult's sweet tooth. These biscotti are my favorite crunchy dessert. I enjoy eating them dipped in vegan hot cocoa (which you can find on my blog). For variety, feel free to experiment with different types of dried fruit and nuts.

1/4 cup grapeseed oil

1/2 cup agave nectar

2 large eggs

1 tablespoon vanilla extract

3 cups blanched almond flour

1/4 teaspoon sea salt

1 teaspoon baking soda

1/2 cup coarsely chopped dark chocolate (73% cacao)

1/2 cup dried cranberries

1/2 cup pecans, coarsely chopped

✧

Preheat the oven to 350°F. Line 2 large baking sheets with parchment paper.

In a large bowl, blend the grapeseed oil, agave nectar, eggs, and vanilla extract with a handheld mixer until frothy, 2 to 3 minutes. In a separate large bowl, combine the almond flour, salt, and baking soda. Stir the wet ingredients into the almond flour mixture until thoroughly combined. Fold in the chocolate, dried cranberries, and pecans. Form the dough into 2 (9 by 3-inch) logs on the prepared baking sheets.

Bake for 25 to 30 minutes, until the logs are brown around the edges. Let the logs cool for 1 hour on the baking sheets.

Transfer the logs to a cutting board. With a serrated knife, cut into 1/2-inch slices on the diagonal. Return the biscotti to the baking sheets.

Bake until crisp, about 16 minutes, turning the slices over midway through. Let the biscotti cool on the baking sheets for 30 minutes, then serve.

Lemon Bars

MAKES 16 BARS ✧ SWEETNESS: HIGH

These lemon bars retain their classic appeal and are just as delicious without the gluten, dairy, and refined sugar.

CRUST

1 1/2 cups blanched almond flour

less 1/2 teaspoon sea salt

2 tablespoons grapeseed oil

1 tablespoon agave nectar

1 tablespoon vanilla extract

TOPPING

1/4 cup grapeseed oil

1/4 cup agave nectar

3 large eggs

1/2 cup freshly squeezed lemon juice

Preheat the oven to 350°F. Grease an 8-inch square baking dish with grapeseed oil and dust with almond flour.

To make the crust, combine the almond flour and salt in a large bowl. In a medium bowl, whisk together the grapeseed oil, agave nectar, and vanilla extract. Stir the wet ingredients into the almond flour mixture until thoroughly combined. Press the dough into the prepared baking dish.

Bake for 15 to 17 minutes, until lightly golden.

While the crust bakes, prepare the topping. In a blender, combine the grapeseed oil, agave nectar, eggs, and lemon juice. Process on high until smooth. Remove the crust from the oven. Pour the topping evenly over the hot crust.

Bake for 15 to 20 minutes, until the topping is golden. Let cool in the baking dish for 30 minutes, then refrigerate for 2 hours to set. Cut into bars and serve.

Raspberry Bars

MAKES 20 BARS ✥ SWEETNESS: HIGH

These bars are a classic. Based on a recipe from *Joy of Cooking*, they are as good as ever, though my version is made without the white sugar, wheat, or butter.

CRUST

3 cups blanched almond flour

1/2 teaspoon sea salt

1/4 cup grapeseed oil

1 tablespoon vanilla extract

TOPPING

1 3/4 cups blanched almond flour

1/4 teaspoon sea salt

1/2 teaspoon ground cinnamon

1/4 cup grapeseed oil

2 tablespoons agave nectar

1 large egg, whisked

1 cup sliced almonds

FILLING

1 cup raspberry fruit spread

Preheat the oven to 350°F. Grease a 13 by 9-inch baking dish with grapeseed oil and dust with almond flour.

To make the crust, blend the almond flour, salt, grapeseed oil, and vanilla extract in a food processor until smooth. Press the dough into the prepared baking dish.

Bake for 12 to 15 minutes, until lightly golden.

While the crust bakes, prepare the topping. In a large bowl, combine the almond flour, salt, and cinnamon. Stir in the grapeseed oil, agave nectar, and egg. Fold in the almond slices.

When the crust is baked, remove it from the oven and distribute the raspberry fruit spread evenly over the hot crust. Distribute the topping evenly over the fruit spread.

Bake for 15 to 20 minutes, until the topping is lightly golden. Let cool in the baking dish for 1 hour. Cut into bars and serve.

Apricot Tea Squares

MAKES 16 SQUARES ❖ SWEETNESS: LOW

For these squares, be sure that your dried apricots are soft and moist (as opposed to hard and dry). It will make all the difference. After cooling, store covered to preserve the chewy texture and apricot flavor of this purely fruit-sweetened dessert.

1 cup dried apricots

1 cup unsweetened shredded coconut, toasted

2 cups blanched almond flour

1/2 teaspoon sea salt

1/4 teaspoon baking soda

1 large egg

1 tablespoon vanilla extract

Preheat the oven to 350°F. Grease an 8-inch square baking dish with grapeseed oil and dust with almond flour.

In a food processor, blend the apricots and coconut until the mixture is crumbly. Pulse in the almond flour, then add the salt, baking soda, egg, and vanilla extract. Blend until well combined. Press the batter into the prepared baking dish.

Bake for 20 to 25 minutes, until firm. Let cool in the baking dish for 1 hour. Cut into squares and serve.

Praline Shortbread Squares

MAKES 16 SQUARES ✛ SWEETNESS: HIGH

This rich, sweet dessert is almost candylike, though still nourishing with a decent dose of high-protein pecans and almond flour.

SHORTBREAD

2 cups blanched almond flour

1/2 teaspoon sea salt

1/4 cup grapeseed oil

1 tablespoon agave nectar

PRALINES

1/2 cup salted butter

1/4 cup agave nectar

1 tablespoon vanilla extract

2 1/4 cups pecans, toasted and coarsely chopped

Preheat the oven to 350°F. Grease an 8-inch square baking dish with grapeseed oil and dust with almond flour.

To make the shortbread, blend the almond flour, salt, grapeseed oil, and agave nectar in a food processor until smooth. Press the dough into the prepared baking dish.

Bake for 15 to 20 minutes, until golden brown. Remove from the oven and let cool.

While the shortbread bakes, prepare the pralines. In a small saucepan over medium-low heat, melt the butter, then add the agave nectar and vanilla extract. Simmer for 5 minutes, then add the pecans. Remove the praline mixture from the heat, cool to room temperature, and spread over the shortbread.

Place in the refrigerator for 3 hours to set. Cut into squares and serve.

Ginger Macadamia Brownies

MAKES 20 BROWNIES ◆ SWEETNESS: HIGH

The spiciness of healing ginger (full of anti-inflammatory compounds and antioxidants) juxtaposed with a double dose of heart-healthy dark chocolate, plus almond flour and macadamia nuts (rich in good monounsaturated fats), makes this dish a nutritional winner.

3 2¹/₂ cups blanched almond flour

¹/₂ teaspoon sea salt

1 teaspoon baking soda

¹/₄ cup unsweetened cocoa powder

¹/₄ cup grapeseed oil

5 2 large eggs

1 cup agave nectar   ¹/₃ c xylitol ³/₄ Tsp stevia

1 tablespoon vanilla extract

¹/₄ cup peeled and minced fresh ginger

1 cup macadamia nuts, coarsely chopped

¹/₂ cup coarsely chopped dark chocolate (73% cacao)

touch of milk

Preheat the oven to 350°F. Grease an 11 by 7-inch baking dish with grapeseed oil and dust with almond flour.

In a large bowl, combine the almond flour, salt, baking soda, and cocoa powder. In a medium bowl, whisk together the grapeseed oil, eggs, agave nectar, vanilla extract, and ginger. Stir the wet ingredients into the almond flour mixture until thoroughly combined. Stir in the macadamia nuts and chocolate. Pour the batter into the prepared baking dish.

Bake for 30 to 35 (25) minutes, until a knife inserted into the center of the dish comes out clean.

Let cool in the baking dish for 1 hour. Cut into bars and serve.

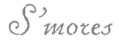

S'mores

MAKES 16 COOKIES ❖ SWEETNESS: HIGH

This quaint classic is now an elegant dessert. To make glorious, party-worthy s'mores, use pastry rings; for a simpler version, use muffin tins.

1³/₄ cups blanched almond flour

¹/₂ teaspoon sea salt

¹/₄ cup grapeseed oil

¹/₂ cup agave nectar

2 tablespoons yacon syrup

1 teaspoon vanilla extract

2 cups coarsely chopped dark chocolate (73% cacao)

1 cup Marshmallow Frosting (page 125)

❖

Preheat the oven to 350°F. Place 16 (2-inch) pastry rings greased with grapeseed oil and dusted with almond flour on a parchment-lined baking sheet. Alternatively, line the bottoms of 16 muffin cups with a circle of parchment paper.

In a large bowl, combine the almond flour and salt. In a medium bowl, whisk together the grapeseed oil, agave nectar, yacon syrup, and vanilla extract. Stir the wet ingredients into the almond flour mixture until thoroughly combined. With damp fingers to prevent sticking, press 1 heaping tablespoon of the dough into each ring or muffin cup.

Bake for 15 minutes, or until dark golden brown. Let cool completely.

Run a small knife around the edges of the pastry rings or muffin cups to loosen the bases.

In a small pan, melt the chocolate over very low heat until smooth. Scoop 1 tablespoon of melted chocolate onto each base and place in the refrigerator for 15 to 20 minutes, until set. Run a knife inside the edge of each ring or muffin cup, then gently pop out the chocolate-covered base.

Allow the S'mores to come to room temperature, then heap 1 tablespoon of Marshmallow Frosting on top of each. Place the S'mores on a pretty platter and serve.

Toppings, Syrups, and Sauces

Cinnamon Apple Syrup

MAKES 3 CUPS ✦ SWEETNESS: HIGH

This thick apple syrup is excellent poured over Pancakes (page 23) or French Toast (page 21), though it is just as good on its own, the way my boys like it. The syrup will thicken as it cools. If necessary, reheat the syrup to return it to its original consistency. Use Braeburn or Gala apples, or try Golden Delicious for a sweeter version; for a hint of tartness, use Granny Smith.

2 cups apple juice

2 medium apples, peeled, cored, and sliced 1/4 inch thick

1 teaspoon ground cinnamon

2 tablespoons arrowroot powder

1/4 cup water

In a large saucepan, bring the apple juice and apples to a boil. Whisk in the cinnamon, then decrease the heat to a simmer for 5 minutes.

In a small bowl, dissolve the arrowroot powder in water, stirring to make a slurry. Raise the heat under the saucepan to high. Add the arrowroot slurry to the apples and stir constantly until the mixture thickens, about 1 minute. Simmer over medium heat for 12 to 15 minutes, until the mixture reaches the consistency of syrup.

Store in a glass Mason jar in the refrigerator for up to 3 days.

Blueberry Sauce

MAKES 1 1/2 CUPS ✦ SWEETNESS: LOW

Blueberries, considered a superfood, are higher in antioxidants than any other fruit. A bowl of this nourishing sauce settles an upset stomach. It's also the perfect topping for Pancakes (page 23), French Toast (page 21), or yogurt.

1 (10-ounce) package frozen blueberries

Pinch of nutmeg

1 tablespoon arrowroot powder

1/4 cup water

In a covered saucepan over medium heat, cook the frozen blueberries and nutmeg for 10 minutes, until the blueberries are soft. In a small bowl, dissolve the arrowroot powder in water, stirring to make a slurry. Raise the heat under the saucepan to high. Add the arrowroot slurry to the blueberries and whisk constantly until the mixture thickens and becomes glossy, about 1 minute. Allow the sauce to cool slightly (and thicken) before serving over your favorite breakfast treat.

Store in a glass Mason jar in the refrigerator for up to 3 days.

Tomato Sauce

MAKES 3 CUPS

I use this tangy tomato sauce for Chicken Parmesan (page 41) and Eggplant Parmesan (page 58). You could also try it over gluten-free pasta. Use a high-quality pure organic tomato paste to take your sauce to a whole new level.

14 ounces tomato paste

2 cups water

1 tablespoon herbes de Provence

1 tablespoon sea salt

1 tablespoon balsamic vinegar

1 tablespoon minced garlic

In a saucepan, bring the tomato paste, water, herbes de Provence, salt, vinegar, and garlic to a boil. Decrease the heat to low, and simmer for 10 to 15 minutes, until the sauce is slightly thicker.

Store in a glass Mason jar in the refrigerator for up to 4 days.

Pizza Sauce

MAKES 1 CUP

Pizza sauce needs to be thicker than tomato sauce in order to keep your crust from getting soggy. This sauce with tasty herbes de Provence does the trick. I keep my pantry stocked with jars of pure organic tomato paste so that I can whip up a quick batch of this sauce (along with a pizza) anytime.

7 ounces tomato paste

$1/4$ cup water

1 tablespoon herbes de Provence

1 teaspoon sea salt

1 tablespoon minced garlic

In a saucepan, bring the tomato paste, water, herbes de Provence, salt, and garlic to a boil. Decrease the heat to low, and simmer for 10 to 15 minutes, until thick.

Spread the sauce over Pizza Crust (page 82) or store in a glass Mason jar in the refrigerator for up to 4 days.

Chocolate Frosting

MAKES 1¹/₂ CUPS ✦ SWEETNESS: HIGH

This vegan chocolate frosting is superb on Very Vanilla Cupcakes (page 94), Chocolate Cake (page 84), or between Chewy Chocolate Cookies (page 102). Be sure to use a 73% cacao chocolate for this recipe to ensure the proper consistency. Studies show that dark chocolate lowers blood pressure and reduces cholesterol. Since this frosting does not contain the usual butter, it is an optimally heart-healthy topping for desserts.

1 cup coarsely chopped dark chocolate (73% cacao)

¹/₂ cup grapeseed oil

2 tablespoons agave nectar

1 tablespoon vanilla extract

Pinch of sea salt

In a medium saucepan over very low heat, melt the chocolate with the grapeseed oil until smooth. Stir in the agave nectar, vanilla extract, and salt.

Place in the freezer for 10 to 15 minutes, until cooled. Remove from the freezer and whip with a handheld mixer until thick and fluffy, 1 to 2 minutes. Use to frost cakes or cupcakes, or as a filling between cookies.

Store in a glass Mason jar in the refrigerator for up to 3 days.

Peanut Butter Frosting

MAKES 1¹/₂ CUPS ✦ SWEETNESS: HIGH

I like to spread this rich and creamy frosting between my Chewy Chocolate Cookies (page 102), or use it as a filling between cake layers when I double my Chocolate Cake recipe (page 84).

1 cup peanut butter

¹/₂ cup agave nectar

¹/₂ teaspoon sea salt

1 teaspoon vanilla extract

In a large bowl, whip the peanut butter and agave nectar together with a handheld mixer until smooth. Blend in the salt and vanilla extract and continue blending until rich and creamy. Use to frost cakes or cupcakes, or as a filling between cookies.

Store in a glass Mason jar in the refrigerator for up to 2 days.

Marshmallow Frosting

MAKES 3 CUPS ✤ SWEETNESS: HIGH

This marshmallow frosting recipe was inspired by one of my favorite cookbook authors, the late Elaine Gottschall. It works especially well with S'mores (page 120) and is divine frosted over Chocolate Cake (page 84) or sandwiched between Chewy Chocolate Cookies (page 102). Don't fear if the mixture overcooks and the agave nectar turns dark amber—you will have a roasted marshmallow frosting, creating a slightly different, though equally tasty, treat.

1/2 cup agave nectar
2 egg whites

In a small saucepan over medium heat, bring the agave nectar to a boil, stirring frequently. Decrease the heat to low and simmer for 4 to 8 minutes, watching constantly and stirring occasionally, until the agave nectar darkens slightly from its original amber color.

In a large bowl, using a handheld mixer, whip the egg whites to stiff peaks. Drizzle the agave nectar slowly into the egg whites, whisking continuously until blended. Use to frost cakes or cupcakes, or as a filling between cookies.

Store in a glass Mason jar in the refrigerator for up to 24 hours.

Creamy Coconut Frosting

MAKES 3 CUPS ✤ SWEETNESS: HIGH

Add organic food coloring to this frosting to create a rainbow of colors.

1/2 1 cup unsweetened coconut milk
1/2 1 cup agave nectar
Pinch of sea salt
1 2 tablespoons arrowroot powder
1/2 1 tablespoon water
1/2 1 1/4 cups coconut oil, melted over very low heat *plus 2 T oil*

In a medium saucepan, bring the coconut milk, agave nectar, and salt to a boil, stirring to combine. Whisk the ingredients together, then decrease the heat and simmer for 8 to 10 minutes, stirring frequently. In a small bowl, dissolve the arrowroot powder in water, stirring to make a paste. Raise the heat under the saucepan to medium-high. Add the arrowroot paste to the coconut mixture, whisking constantly until the mixture thickens, about 1 minute. Remove the pan from the heat, and very gradually blend in the coconut oil with a handheld mixer until smooth.

Place in the freezer for 30 to 35 minutes, until the frosting solidifies and turns an opaque white. Remove from the freezer and whip with a handheld mixer until thick and fluffy. Use to frost cakes or cupcakes, or as a filling between cookies.

Store in a glass Mason jar in the refrigerator for up to 3 days.

Whipped Cream

MAKES 4 CUPS ◆ SWEETNESS: MEDIUM

I used to think whipped cream was a food group in and of itself before I cut back on my dairy intake. This Whipped Cream is a cloud of perfection on Pecan Pie (page 68) and Pumpkin Pie (page 70), or for a very decadent breakfast, on top of Pancakes (page 23). Fun and easy to make, this is a great first recipe to teach your children—just be sure not to overwhip your cream or you will have homemade butter!

2 cups heavy cream
2 tablespoons agave nectar
1 tablespoon vanilla extract

In a deep bowl, whip the cream, agave nectar, and vanilla extract with a handheld mixer for 2 to 3 minutes, until thick, fluffy, and firm.

Store in a glass Mason jar in the refrigerator for up to 24 hours.

Crème Pâtissière

MAKES 1½ CUPS ◆ SWEETNESS: HIGH

Some say this is a culinary miracle—pastry crème without heavy cream, milk, or eggs. My cholesterol-counting friends are more than happy to test desserts made with this rich, vegan, guilt-free Crème Pâtissière.

1 cup cashews
1 cup plus 1 tablespoon water
1/3 cup agave nectar
1 tablespoon vanilla extract
1 tablespoon arrowroot powder

In a blender, puree the cashews, 1 cup of the water, agave nectar, and vanilla extract on the highest setting for 1 to 2 minutes, until smooth. Place the cashew mixture in a medium saucepan and bring to a boil. Whisk constantly for 1 minute, then decrease the heat to a simmer while preparing the arrowroot paste.

In a small bowl, dissolve the arrowroot powder in the remaining 1 tablespoon of water, stirring to make a paste. Increase the heat to high and add the arrowroot paste to the cashew mixture, whisking constantly for about 1 minute, until the mixture thickens. Remove from the heat.

Store in a glass Mason jar in the refrigerator for up to 2 days.

Sources

AGAR FLAKES

Eden Foods
888-424-3336
www.edenfoods.com

AGAVE NECTAR

Madhava
303-823-5166
www.madhavasagave.com

ALMOND FLOUR

Honeyville
888-810-3212
www.honeyvillegrain.com

Lucy's Kitchen Shop
888-484-2126
www.lucyskitchenshop.com

Nuts Online
800-558-6887
www.nutsonline.com

ARROWROOT POWDER

More Than Alive
800-516-5911
www.morethanalive.com

CHOCOLATE
(chocodrops, cocoa powder)

Dagoba Chocolate
800-393-6075
www.dagobachocolate.com

COCONUT FLOUR

Wilderness Family Naturals
800-945-3801
www.wildernessfamilynaturals.com

FRUIT SPREAD

Rigoni di Asiago
858-605-1898
www.homenaturalsinc.com

FiordiFrutta
541-899-1047
www.jacksonvillemercantile.com

LOAF PAN
(7.5 by 3.5 by 2.25 inches)

Magic Line
866-716-2433
www.cheftools.com

OIL
(coconut, grapeseed)

Spectrum Naturals
800-434-4246
www.spectrumorganics.com

SALT
(finely ground Celtic Sea Salt)

Selina Naturally
800-867-7258
www.celticseasalt.com

SPICES
(All Purpose Chef's Shake seasoning, herbes de Provence)

Spice Hunter
800-444-3061
www.spicehunter.com

TOMATO PASTE

Bionaturae
520-792-0804
www.shoporganic.com

VANILLA EXTRACT

Flavorganics
973-344-8014
www.flavorganics.com

YACON SYRUP

Navitas Naturals
888-645-4282
www.navitasnaturals.com

Notes

1. Peter Green, *Celiac Disease: A Hidden Epidemic* (New York: HarperCollins, 2006).

2. Represents the glycemic indexes of white bread and white rice (GI not available for grain flours).

    See Dr. Jennie Brand-Miller et al., *The New Glucose Revolution: The Authoritative Guide to the Glycemic Index—the Dietary Solution for Lifelong Health* (New York: Marlowe & Company, 1999).

3. U.S. Department of Agriculture—Agricultural Research Service, Nutrient Database, "Nutrition Information: nuts, almonds, blanched," www.nal.usda .gov/fnic/foodcomp/search/.

4. Ibid., "Nutrition Information: wheat flour, white."

5. Ibid., "Nutrition Information: rice flour, white."

6. Ibid., "Nutrition information: nuts, almonds, blanched."

7. Ibid., "Nutrition information: wheat flour, white."

8. Ibid., "Nutrition information: rice flour, white."

9. University of Sydney: Home of the Glycemic Index, International GI Database, "Glycemic Index, Sugar," www.glycemicindex.com.

10. Ibid., "Glycemic Index, Maple Syrup."

11. Ibid., "Glycemic Index, Honey."

12. Madhava, Inc., Madhava Agave Nutrition Information, "Glycemic Index, Agave Nectar," www.madhavasagave.com/aboutagave.aspx.

Index